# PROFESSIONAL PRACTICE SCHOOLS

## Linking Teacher Education and School Reform

# PROFESSIONAL PRACTICE SCHOOLS

## Linking Teacher Education and School Reform

EDITED BY
## Marsha Levine

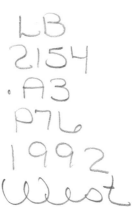

TEACHERS
COLLEGE
PRESS

Teachers College, Columbia University
New York and London

Published by Teachers College Press, 1234 Amsterdam Avenue
New York, NY 10027

*Library of Congress Cataloging-in-Publication Data*

Professional practice schools : linking teacher education and school reform / edited by
    Marsha Levine.
        p.        cm.
    Includes bibliographical references and index.
    ISBN 0-8077-3176-5 (alk. paper). —ISBN 0-8077-3175-7 (pbk. : alk. paper)
    1. Laboratory schools—United States.   2. Student teaching—United
States.   3. Teachers—Training of—United States.   4. Educational change—United
States.   I. Levine, Marsha.
LB2154.A3P76       1992
370'.7'33—dc20

Printed on acid-free paper

Manufactured in the United States of America

99  98  97  96  95  94  93  92      8  7  6  5  4  3  2  1

# Contents

# Foreword

Public education in modern America has been a big success and a big failure. Our system of universal education has helped us to create one society out of the diverse groups that make up our nation, and it continues to do this. On the other hand, we are finding it woefully inadequate to the challenges of the new global economy. Our students do not have the skills they need to make the United States competitive in world markets. If we wish to continue to be world leaders and to live in a prosperous society, we must remake our education system.

What does this mean? It means starting from scratch and thinking about exactly what we want our students to know and be able to do. It means looking at the way youngsters learn and teachers teach. And it means looking at the structures and institutions that make up our education system so we can redesign them in ways that will raise the achievement of all our students and give our country the world-class education system we need.

We've been thinking about these issues at the American Federation of Teachers (AFT), and the work in school restructuring and teacher education presented in this volume is part of the result.

We believe that all kids can learn—though they learn at different rates and in different ways—and we believe they are entitled to equal opportunities to do so. We know there is a big difference between learning in school and out of school. And we think we know the kinds of classrooms and schools that would help all students become workers engaged in the job of learning.

Creating these new classrooms and schools will be a big job. But the work doesn't stop there because we also will need teachers to teach in our restructured schools. Where will they come from and how will we educate them?

The answer is that most teachers who are going to teach in a restructured school will need to learn in one. People tend to teach the way they themselves have been taught, and most of us have grown up in schools where teaching means chalk and talk—standing up in front of the class and telling students what they are supposed to know. So it's important that teachers who are going to work in restructured schools have a chance to see and practice the kind of teaching that will go on in these new schools.

The problem is that we do not now have schools where teachers can undertake internships of this kind. But when there is no institution to answer an important need, people have to invent one. The professional practice school, an idea we have borrowed from the medical profession's teaching hospitals, is one answer to how we can educate teachers to work in restructured schools.

It was not always like this. Teaching hospitals emerged at a critical time in the history of the medical profession and the history of the hospital as an institution. Training for young doctors was haphazard, and there were no standards for medical practice or, indeed, for hospitals. Teaching hospitals played a very important role in the development of the standards of medical training and medical practice. And they are still the only places where it is acceptable for young doctors to do the clinical training that is required for their certification.

Public education is now facing the kind of challenge the medical profession faced earlier in this century. And we believe that the time is right for the invention of an institution that could have the impact on teaching and on schools that teaching hospitals have had on medical practice and hospitals.

Since we began work at the AFT designing such an institution, the professional practice school, important changes have taken place. Increasingly, public schools see that they must transform themselves if they are to survive. Important work done by John Goodlad and members of the Holmes Group has emphasized the link between school change and teacher education. Foundation-supported projects have sprung up to begin creating what are variously called clinical schools, professional development schools, and professional practice schools.

The AFT is grateful for Exxon Education Foundation's continuing support as we have thought about what professional practice schools should be and worked to begin implementing our ideas at several pilot sites. With the publication of this volume, these ideas will be made even more accessible to those who are interested in serious school restructuring.

Albert Shanker
President,
American Federation of Teachers

# PROFESSIONAL PRACTICE SCHOOLS

## Linking Teacher Education and School Reform

# Introduction

## MARSHA LEVINE

*In 1988 the American Federation of Teachers, with support from Exxon Education Foundation, established a task force to address the broad question of how to prepare teachers for restructured schools. Specifically, its purpose was to envision what a restructured school with responsibility for clinical teacher education might look like. The chapters in this volume were written to help bring clarity to some of the key issues in the design and implementation of such institutions, which have come to be called "professional practice schools."*

This is a time when attention is focused on the failure of America's schools to meet the needs of our society as it moves into the twenty-first century. Concern has naturally and correctly gravitated toward the quality of our teaching force and the adequacy of their preparation to do the job at hand. Predictably, activity in the school reform movement and that in the teacher education arena have not converged. School folks and university people have always had some difficulty communicating. What has been happening is not so unusual. Teacher educators have been trying to fix their end of the problem with efforts to improve how teachers are prepared. School people have been trying to remedy the problem with numerous efforts to redesign their schools and school districts. Professional practice schools may provide a common ground in which teacher education and school reform can come together to achieve the end result of improving student learning.

Numerous efforts are underway to improve the preparation of teachers by enhancing the student teaching or internship experience. The idiosyncratic nature of this requirement in teacher education, coupled with the importance placed on it by virtually all practicing teachers, has led to the establishment of various models for clinical schools, professional development schools, and training schools, all of which are attempting to bring structure and standards to this part of a teacher's education. Many of these have a collaborative governance structure, and they often reflect

1

the notion that practitioners should have more responsibility for the clinical education of new teachers. While these efforts may vastly improve clinical training and contribute to the growing professionalization of teaching, it does not automatically follow that schools will therefore be better simply because the new teachers entering them have been better trained. It means only that the teachers may be better trained to function in schools as they are today. Improved teacher practice will still be individual, bureaucratic, and based on a narrow interpretation of the teacher's role. In order for these improvements in clinical teacher education to make a difference in terms of student success, it is the conclusion of the AFT task force that they also must be linked to efforts to change the schools themselves.

Professional practice schools create these links. They are restructured public schools with responsibility for teacher education. They also are designed to support ongoing research directed at improving practice. The term *professional practice school* refers both to the nature of practice in the school and to the function of the site as a place where novices *practice* their skills and use what they have learned in preparing to become teachers. The term was chosen to emphasize the relationship between school reform and teacher education.

## TEACHING AND LEARNING IN RESTRUCTURED SCHOOLS

Restructured schools are defined by a fundamentally different conception of both teaching and learning. Where traditional schools are structured to support a rather passive kind of learning in which knowledge is transferred from teacher to student, learning in restructured schools is defined as an active process in which the learner constructs meaning out of experience. The teacher's role then becomes more that of a facilitator or designer of the experiences and environment to promote such learning. What does it mean to help students learn to use their minds well? What is active learning? What does it mean for students to construct meaning? And what does all that imply for how teachers practice? Students engaged with both content and their peers require a very different role to be played by their teachers. Not only do instructional strategies change but teachers must become involved in doing things not common in bureaucratic schools.

Engaging students in active learning directed at deep knowledge of content and the development of thinking and problem-solving skills will require reflective, analytical, inquiring teacher practice. Teaching will no longer be mostly telling; the teacher will become the coach, questioner, organizer, the one who frames and solves problems, judges, compares, observes, inquires, and consults. Among the teaching strategies used will be group problem solving, peer teaching, cooperative learning, reciprocal teaching, and project work involving real consequences. Instead of listening and recalling, students will, as Pechman writes in Chapter 2, invent, explain, and elaborate, extend their thinking, and defend their positions.

In addition, teachers will assume new responsibilities school-wide. They will collaboratively evaluate and review practice in their schools; focus on the individual and collective needs of students in faculty-wide forums; take on such organizational functions as grading policies, student and teacher assignments, organization of instruction, curriculum design, resource allocation, and scheduling (see Chapter 4). They will do these things because these are the dimensions that affect the quality of teaching and learning in schools, and the practitioners' informed judgment must be a part of making decisions in these areas.

The professional practice school is the place where new teachers will learn these new roles. They will be trained and socialized into these new settings, expectations, and norms for schooling in restructured schools that have deliberately assumed the responsibility for teacher education. Numerous efforts toward restructuring schools are underway throughout the country. Few, if any, have given serious attention to the question of how to educate teachers for these new and different roles. Without a deliberate effort to educate new teachers and induct them into transformed schools, the efforts of the committed few will almost certainly have little impact on the broader community of schools and on the development of professional practice in teaching. Restructuring without attention to teacher education and induction is probably doomed to a narrow and parochial existence. The converse, development of clinical schools with no link to restructuring, is equally flawed; it will, perhaps, produce better ways to educate teachers for the schools we have, but will have little influence in improving the quality of public education. It is difficult to imagine significant change occurring in public education while the clinical education of teachers remains a mirror of the existing school model and a powerful way of reinforcing it.

## EXPLORING THE DIMENSIONS AND ISSUES IN PROFESSIONAL PRACTICE SCHOOLS

The authors in this book were asked to consider various aspects of the design of professional practice schools. They explored several dimensions, including the philosophical, political, practical, and intellectual domains. Among the questions that guided their exploration were the following:

- What is the nature of the student's experience?
- What constitutes professional practice for teachers and how does the school as an organization support that practice?
- What do new teachers have to learn about teaching in restructured schools and how will they learn those things?
- Is there a conflict between professional accountability and public accountability?
- What are the standards by which a school might be judged qualified to take on this responsibility?
- What is the special role professional practice schools may play in establishing standards for practice and for the institutions (schools) in which practice takes place?
- What are the policy and inter-institutional barriers that will make it difficult to in fact implement professional practice schools?

In Chapter 1 I present the conceptual framework for restructured schools with responsibility for teacher training and practice-based research. The progressive roots of these institutions are traced uniquely through the work of Abraham Flexner, father of the modern teaching hospital. The analogy of the teaching hospital is discussed as the characteristics of the two institutions are compared and contrasted. The basic assumptions on which the professional practice school is designed are identified, and the characteristics that exemplify the basic values and purposes of the institution are described. It is this basic framework that the various authors used as their points of departure for examining the various dimensions of the professional practice school.

Ellen Pechman in Chapter 2 begins with the conception of the professional practice school as described in Chapter 1. She then poses several questions aimed at uncovering why such a place, so designed, would be good for children. She asks what we know about children coming to school today: Who are they; how do they learn; what do we know about their social and emotional development? Following an excellent synthesis of the literature related to these questions, she explores the implications for the way schools are organized, the way teachers teach, and the way teachers learn. The research and analysis she presents lead to the conclusions that (1) schools need to be different from what they are now; and (2) the design of the professional practice school is consistent with what we know about learners.

What do intern or student teachers have to learn, and how will they learn it? These are the questions that frame Chapter 3. Mary Kennedy looks at professional practice in other fields to identify the kinds of expertise that are encompassed and how each uses knowledge or content in a different way. The four kinds of expertise she identifies are: (1) the application of skills; (2) the application of technical concepts or theories; (3) the ability to "critically analyze a situation and generate multiple interpretations of it"; and (4) the ability to take action on the basis of critical analysis that involves selecting goals from a range of possibilities, which then serve as a screen for choosing action. The last can be learned only in real situations through real experiences, and that is what Kennedy concentrates on as the curriculum of the professional practice school for student teachers. Kennedy draws implications for the professional practice school from this analysis of professional practice.

Professional practice schools are not only schools where novices learn to teach, they are also, as Linda Darling-Hammond explains in Chapter 4, "schools intended to promote professional practice in teaching." As such they have a special role to play in establishing standards that can become a part of a useful professional accountability structure. They have an important role in defining meaningful standards of practice; in creating reasonable means for upholding these standards; and in dealing with ways in which problems surrounding professional practice can be reasonably dealt with by providing vehicles for redress or corrections. Further, they have a responsibility to set and maintain standards that will ensure that all practitioners are adequately prepared. Darling-Hammond concludes by addressing the challenge of meeting both the needs of the students and the needs of the learning teachers in a professional practice school. She describes how this seeming dilemma can be dealt with in the reorganization of schooling and the development of structures designed to achieve both goals.

The concept of professional practice schools embraces the idea of continuous growth and development of teachers through the examination of practice, inquiry and reflection, and collegial problem solving. In Chapter 5 Ann Lieberman and Lynne Miller address this dimension of professional practice schools. They build on a concept of professional practice, maintaining that teachers themselves are an important source of knowledge about teaching, and equating the renewal of teaching with the renewal of schools. *Teacher development,* their preferred term for professional growth activities, means varied activities that are always directed at continuous inquiry and the improvement of teaching. The authors offer a framework for developing a school culture that will support such inquiry, and they identify the problems and dilemmas that exist in creating it.

The institutionalization of professional practice is a core purpose of professional practice schools. In order for this to occur standards for such schools must be developed. This may take some time, but it begins with the recognition of need. In Chapter 6 Holly Houston begins that process. She constructs what she refers to as a "building code" or framework of values that may translate into institutional standards for such schools. The author identifies four basic values that align with the characteristics of a profession and with the mission of the professional practice school. Houston suggests that specific indicators could be identified, examined, and evaluated in a school that would provide evidence of the existence of these values. She suggests what some indicators might be but argues the need for extensive discussion about them. Houston reminds the reader of the important relationship between the development of professional practice in medicine and the development of the teaching hospital, designed to be an institutional base for good practice. She foresees an analogous role for the professional practice school in the development of professional practice in teaching.

If professional practice schools are to be more than design exercises it is necessary to deal with issues that will affect their implementation. In Chapter 7 Barbara Neufeld tackles three areas of critical importance: collaboration among institutions; alternative definitions of teaching and learning; and issues embedded in the policy context in which these institutions will develop.

The creation of collaborative institutions will mean changes for all participants, who will have to rethink what they believe about the nature and sources of knowledge about teaching and learning to teach. Each will have to examine the incentive structures that govern people's behavior. Each will have to assist individuals in learning new roles and assuming new responsibilities.

In the broader policy context, professional practice schools will be created in pre-existing environments characterized by policies that define teaching in ways that are perhaps different from the philosophy underlying professional practice schools. Through examples of various existing policies, Neufeld provides a framework for others to use in examining the context in which they are working to sort out what is supportive to the effort and what changes might be pursued.

Collectively, the authors make the case for a new institution—the professional practice school—that has important roles to play in the transformation of our public schools. As restructured schools, they can serve as exemplars or models of good practice and of institutions that support good practice. As clinical training sites, they will educate and socialize teachers for new roles in restructured schools. And, as institutions dedicated to practice-based research, they will generate an important part of the knowledge base needed to support the ongoing improvement of teaching and learning in our schools.

The chapters in this volume are about restructured schools and teacher education. They focus on the rationale for bringing these worlds together and the issues that arise when that happens. In a sense teacher education has always been a mirror of schooling—professional practice schools may be the places where one can see the reflections of school reform.

# 1 | A Conceptual Framework for Professional Practice Schools

## MARSHA LEVINE

In a 1967 John Dewey Lecture, Robert Schaefer, then Dean of Teachers College, Columbia University, described a vision of schools as centers of inquiry. He maintained that schools where teachers themselves were learning were likely to be places where students would not only learn, but also "learn how to learn." This symbiotic relationship between teaching and learning is central to the concept of a restructured school.

In that 1967 lecture, Schaefer also argued powerfully for the professionalization of teaching. To build and maintain a center of inquiry, teachers needed to learn with and from one another; they needed to be guided by some standard of ethics in their practice; and they needed to be able to draw on some systematic body of knowledge. Schools that could support such practice would have certain characteristics. Schools that were responsible for inducting new teachers would have these characteristics as well. Such schools might be called professional practice schools.

### PROGRESSIVE ROOTS

The professionalization of teaching and the school as a center of inquiry both have roots in the progressive education movement. Schaefer's ideas reach back to those of John Dewey and Lucy Sprague Mitchell. Dewey conceived of teachers as "students of teaching" who should and could reflect on their own practice and learn from one another. Perrone (1989) traces the development of these ideas through Dewey's work and the work of Mitchell at the Bureau of Educational Experiments and Bank Street College (see Mitchell, 1950). In this view, teachers' documentation, records, and reflections are important sources of knowledge about learning and the environments that influence learning. This concept of teaching as research is extended further in the work of Eleanor Duckworth. Based on the belief that learning is a process of making meaning, teaching

8

is defined as the process of uncovering how, and under what conditions, the learner learns (Duckworth, 1986, 1987).

Many analogies have been drawn between the role of the teaching hospital in the practice of medicine and in the reform of hospitals, and the potential of the professional practice school to professionalize teaching and provide a model for institutions that support good practice. It is interesting therefore to find that Abraham Flexner, father of the modern teaching hospital, was himself influenced by John Dewey's philosophy and was directly concerned with elementary and secondary education. In fact the link between the progressive movement and the concept of professional practice schools can be drawn through Flexner's work. In a history of American medicine Ludmerer (1985) describes the influence of John Dewey's progressive philosophy on Flexner's conceptualization of the teaching hospital in the reform of modern medical education. The importance of teaching and learning in clinical settings and the importance of the relationship between research and practice derive from Dewey's conception of the role of knowledge, experience, and practice in the development of the "thinking" individual. The "thinking" individual is defined as one who can analyze, synthesize and make knowledge-based decisions, and has the skills to carry them out (Dewey, 1904/1974).

Flexner's interest in the application of these principles extended from medical education quite literally to elementary and secondary education. In *The Transformation of the School* (1961), Lawrence Cremin describes Flexner's role in the creation of the Lincoln School at Teachers College in 1917. The Lincoln School was an experimental private school that depended heavily on the teachers' involvement in curriculum design and implementation. The philosophy that guided the progressives in education required a trust in the ability of teachers to play a "thinking" role in the planning, development, and implementation of the educational environment and program. The teachers at the Lincoln School did that.

The principles at the heart of the progressive movement—"an abiding commitment to universal education and a profound faith in the average classroom teacher" (Cremin, 1961, p. 299)—are embedded in today's efforts to restructure schools. The context in which we are trying to implement them, however, is different. The obstacles to their implementation are the litany of problems that beset the public schools and an accumulation of efforts that have attempted to legislate and regulate teaching. Underlying the status quo is a notion of teaching that is technical or bureaucratic, a static notion of knowledge, and a passive view of learning. Creating schools that embody the principles of the restructured school will require building from a foundation of beliefs that are quite different from those on which our schools are based today.

## BASIC ASSUMPTIONS UNDERLYING PROFESSIONAL PRACTICE SCHOOLS

The design of an institution like the professional practice school begins with an explicit statement of beliefs and values. Underlying the model described in this volume are a set of assumptions about teaching, learning, knowledge, and schooling. What are these cornerstones, and what must be said about them from the beginning?

### Learning and Knowing

Underlying the professional practice school is a definition of learning that embraces the notions that there are many different ways of knowing and that learning is essentially an active process.

A school built on these assumptions defines roles, for both students and teachers, different from those in traditional schools. There are, for example, expectations for performance based on what is learned. Students and teachers are expected to use what they have learned and are expected to learn how to learn. Relationships among student, teacher, and the curriculum are different. In place of the teacher as imparter of wisdom, the teacher becomes a facilitator of student learning, playing the role of the intermediary in helping the student to negotiate the curriculum. In Chapter 2 Pechman describes in detail the cognitive, developmental, and social bases for these changes and what they in fact look like in the actual school setting.

### Teaching Practice

Max Weber expounded on the concept of bureaucracy and its demand for a corps of technical experts to do the work and manage such institutions. Indeed, bureaucratic schools are best served by teachers who have been trained to function as technical experts. Many teacher education programs are designed to develop such a professional teacher corps. In contrast, the role of the teacher embedded in the restructured school, as envisioned by Dewey, elaborated on by Schaefer, and more recently promoted by many school reform advocates, is not merely a technical expert who uses knowledge but an individual who transforms a knowledge base, reflects on practice, and generates new knowledge.

The traditional view of teaching assumes a linear and hierarchical relationship between scientific knowledge and practice, which is also reflected in the relationship between teacher and learner. In other words, the practitioner's role is to take the findings of scientifically based research and employ them in practice. Research precedes practice. The practitioner is either a user of research or the subject of it. There are two major difficulties with this conception of practice. First, it does not provide for the contribution of the practitioner. Teachers are expected to use theories and findings. It does not call upon them to transform those findings for real situations, which are often indeterminate and uncertain; and it does not provide for the contribution of experience to professional practice other than in its effect on making the practitioner a better user of research. Second, this view does not take into account the role of ethics and values in defining professional practice; most assuredly, teaching is a value-laden profession.

The contrasting view of teaching relies on the concept of reflective practice and the teacher as researcher. In his discussions of reflective practice, Schön (1983, 1987) describes practice as beginning with a knowledge base but then becoming an active process involving inquiry, creativity, analysis, and evaluation, all of which are guided by a set of values or a system of ethics. It is a process that allows the teacher to deal with divergent situations in a value-laden context. "Reflection-in-action," the term Schön gives to this process, is really doing research in practice. The practitioner constructs a new theory for the unique case he or she is confronting. This kind of action is a kind of experimenting and can develop a rigor of its own. Inquiry and action come together in reflective practice. It is the essence of "teacher as researcher."

The education of such a practitioner is the concern of the professional practice school.

## An Ethical Base for Professional Practice

Professions, by definition, have a moral structure that is meant to guide the professional's actions. Professionals must agree to uphold this moral structure. The school as an institution ought to support that moral structure. The professional practice school is the place where professionals learn what that structure means in action.

A starting place for developing a moral structure or system of ethics for the practice of education might appropriately be those values that are embedded in education in a democracy. Although they may give rise to varied interpretation and implications, they can reflect a set of core values that can become the basis for the development of standards in the professional practice school. The values should guide professional behavior with respect to students, the profession, and society. The following are suggested as a starting point for discussion and evolution of such a system of ethics:

- Teachers should act in the best interests of their students. They should act in ways to support student success. Their behaviors should be informed by the best knowledge available.
- Teachers should uphold the standards of the profession for themselves and for others. They should not misrepresent themselves or their qualifications for practice.
- Teachers should be committed to the maintenance of democratic values in the settings in which they teach, including fairness, decency, justice, and equity.

These core values would also be used to measure the appropriateness of other actions that are taken in the name of education, that is, state mandates, local district regulations, textbook development, and curriculum development.

Ethical behavior, however, is determined not solely by an explicitly stated moral code. Mary Kennedy (1987) points out that an additional source for defining ethical behavior is the social norms of the school culture. The significance of the professional practice school in this respect is its ability to model the norms of practice that uphold the ethical standards defined by the profession. It is the consistency between the professional standards and "the way things are done around here" that is so unique and important.

## Summary

Thus, the basic assumptions that underlie the professional practice school (and that guided the authors in the development of their chapters in this book) have to do with a vision of learning, a view of professional teaching, and the responsibilities of public education. In summary these assumptions are

1. The primary goal of schools is to support student academic and social learning.
2. Learning is an active process that occurs in different ways and at different rates.
3. Professional practice in teaching is knowledge-based, reflective, and inquiring.
4. Public schools are obligated to safeguard both equity and high standards for learning outcomes.

In laying out these assumptions, or beliefs, they become the screens through which all decisions must pass about the structure of the professional practice school and what goes on within it. It should be noted that these are the assumptions that undergird restructured schools generally. The fact that the professional practice school takes on the additional responsibilities of clinical teacher education and support of practice-based research necessitates two additional assumptions.

5. The environment that supports teacher learning will also support student learning; that is, the professional practice school is a community of learners.
6. If one hopes to have teachers teach in different ways, one must change the way teachers are themselves taught.

## THE ORGANIZATIONAL BASE FOR PROFESSIONAL PRACTICE

Professions are normally characterized by a knowledge base, a moral framework, and a collegial structure. The institution in which practice takes place ought to support these features; the traditional school does not. The characteristics of the professional practice school are designed to do this. The governance and organization of the professional practice school should support teachers as the ultimate authority on conditions that affect professional practice, just as doctors oversee decisions affecting medical practice in a hospital. This includes a shared decision-making process among faculty and administration on questions of both policy and practice, with the faculty in control on instructional questions. Collegiality is encouraged by the way in which time is allocated to permit opportunities for frequent and ongoing communication, observation and feedback between peers, joint planning, and peer teaching among faculty members. These features, identified by Judith Little (1982), support collegiality as a norm. Professional accountability, in which teachers are responsible to each other for student outcomes, is supported through opportunities for public practice, joint planning, and review of practice. Assessment procedures extend beyond standardized achievement tests, to include profiles of expectations, measures of congruence between expectations and achievement, enrollment patterns, attendance patterns, dropout rates, and exhibits of student learning. Support for reflective teaching is provided through allocation and use of resources (time, facilities, materials, consultants) to encourage a continuous examination of practice. Teachers are assisted in this process through appropriate record-keeping systems, which are maintained for their use.

The institution must be flexible enough to accommodate the teachers' deliberations, consultations, and innovations. Schön (1983) identifies the following characteristics of institutions that support this. There must be flexibility in student groupings and teacher–student ratios to accommodate different learning needs. There needs to be peer interaction among teachers to allow them to communicate their thinking to one another and get feedback from their peers. Reflective practice requires that teachers know how their students think and what influences them to behave in the ways they do. The traditional school functions with a centrally controlled and administered system of accountability and with evaluation that is highly quantitative and seeks to be objective. Reflective practice requires more independent, qualitative, and narrative accounts of progress. Supervision in a professional practice school would focus less on controlling or monitoring and more on supporting and enabling (Schön, 1983, p. 270). In reflective practice teachers are truly inquirers. Students, no longer viewed as receptacles for knowledge, become more responsible for their own learning.

## THE KNOWLEDGE BASE FOR PROFESSIONAL PRACTICE

What should people learn in professional practice schools? What should they already know when they enter? How should assessments of their knowledge be made? Embedded in these questions is a set of issues that educators and the broader community have wrestled with for centuries. What is a good teacher? What does a good teacher have to know? How do teachers learn? We must turn to two bodies of knowledge for the answers that have been given. Both are incomplete and inadequate, but they represent the range of knowledge from which we must build the professional practice school curriculum.

### What Is the Knowledge Base for Teaching?

What does a teacher need to know in order to be effective? That ought to depend on what one wants the teacher to be able to do. Answers to this question range from: A teacher just has to be very well educated, to A teacher must have an undergraduate major in education with a specific number of credits in pedagogy, foundations, and methods.

In her site visits to 20 teacher education programs, Amarel (1987) found that most teacher education programs she looked at identified a common set of categories that were considered a part of the knowledge base of teachers. These included (1) subject-matter knowledge; (2) empirical research, which included effective teaching research; (3) social science and humanities for content on schools and society; (4) knowledge of models of teaching, conceptual schemes, and theoretical constructs of teaching; and (5) knowledge of whatever the state mandated as required teacher education. These were identified by teacher educators involved largely with the academic preparation of teachers. They constitute the range of knowledge that might be considered prerequisite to clinical teacher education. It is important to note Amarel's observation that there is little emphasis on classroom management, grouping, or teacher beliefs in the empirical research. Important aspects of pedagogy for restructured schools, including cooperative group teaching, peer tutoring, reciprocal teaching, and coaching, are presumably little in evidence as well. These are the areas teacher educators identify; implicit in their response is an unspoken but strong conceptualization of the teacher's role.

If one were to conceptualize the research bases that one might want for the student in a professional practice school, the following categories might be useful. The first category would be what we know about how individuals, and specifically children, learn. The second area is what we have learned about the conditions that support learning, including the research on effective schools and effective teaching and especially those pedagogies that are related to teaching in restructured school environments (e.g., cooperative group learning, use of educational technologies, peer tutoring, and coaching).

A third distinct research base, important to the practitioner, is growing out of an examination of the pedagogical requirements of specific content areas. This research focuses on identifying the effective ways of teaching the main understandings or concepts of a particular subject area, such as physics or history.

Teacher interns entering the professional practice school may be expected to have this knowledge base as well as to be prepared in the subject areas they will be teaching. To be able to use it, however, they must be able to "learn in action." "Learning in action" is a particular kind of professional expertise; and for knowledge of how to develop this, we must turn to another area, that of educating professionals and what we know about that.

## What Is Known About Professional Education?

Mary Kennedy's (1987) review of the professional education literature led her to isolate four types of expertise that may be the goal of a professional education. The fields she looked into were medicine, law, engineering, and architecture. The kinds of expertise were: (1) skills or technical abilities; (2) application of general principles and theory; (3) critical analysis; and (4) reflection, or what Kennedy calls deliberate action. A given profession may emphasize one kind of expertise over another. Law, for example, concentrates on critical analysis in the education of new lawyers; architecture emphasizes deliberate action.

It is in focusing on the latter kind of expertise—that of the reflective practitioner—that the professional practice school is unique. How does one develop this ability, these habits of mind, these sensitivities? To do that, the teacher intern must develop the skills of what Shulman (1986) calls strategic analysis, or Schön (1983) describes as reflective inquiry. To help the novice begin to do this is the function of the professional practice school. Schön identifies a set of conditions that must be in place for the professional to engage in reflective practice. These conditions create a common ground for inquiry and communication. They include common language that is used to describe reality and to conduct inquiry; commonly held ways of assessing reality; and recognized, overreaching theories that are used to make sense out of phenomena. Further, there must be what Schön (1983) calls "role frames," which practitioners use to determine what they will do and to define the boundaries of the settings in which they work.

Some work has already begun in preparing teachers for reflective practice. An example is the findings of Zeichner and Liston (1987), at the University of Wisconsin, in working with student teachers. However, those efforts are seriously hampered by the lack of a supportive institutional context for the development of reflective practice. Reflective practice requires collegial interaction and a structure that supports inquiry. It cannot be developed or sustained in isolation. The developers of professional practice schools will have to bear these requirements in mind as they create these institutions. That is the challenge.

## IMPLICATIONS FOR EDUCATING TEACHERS

Since reflective practice defines a broader arena of usable knowledge than scientifically based professional knowledge, educating the professional must go beyond the transmission of scientific technical knowledge and the training in skill to use it. Schön (1983) suggests that kinds of knowing in professional practice include the art of problem framing, the art of implementation, and the art of improvisation. Taken together they affect the way the individual practitioner handles situations that are uncertain, indeterminate, unique, and conflict ridden.

Some professional schools—business, law, and medicine, specifically—have endeavored to help the professional learn to "think like a doctor or think like a lawyer." Professional knowledge, to Schön, and I would agree, goes beyond that. Thinking like a teacher, or thinking like a lawyer, implies a closed system. A right way is presumed. Although this might be a beginning, it cannot be the end. It will not be sufficient for professional practice. The ability to think divergently is essential and is what makes the difference. The relationship between the professional knowledge taught in schools and this "knowing in action" is not clear. What is clear is that one assumes the other. The knowledge base for professional practice as it has been identified in the American Association of Colleges of Teacher Education project, Knowledge Base for Beginning Teachers (Reynolds, 1989), might be thought of as a prerequisite to a focus on the development of reflective practice.

## Characteristics of the Clinical Education Experience

The current model for clinical teacher education programs is grounded in a conceptualization of teaching as a craft. The practice teaching experience is designed for the novice to observe and imitate the experienced teacher. Through repeated practice, it is presumed that the learner will get it right. The cooperating, or mentor, teacher is expected to be able to pass down to the student teacher those "tricks of the trade" that will ensure success in the classroom. It is essentially an apprenticeship model that has been in use in teacher education since the seventeenth century. The apprenticeship model emphasizes the mentor or model teacher rather than the intellectual work of teaching. It is, as Linda Darling-Hammond has pointed out, idiosyncratic and necessarily limited. (For a discussion of student teaching for professional practice, see Stones, 1987.) Teaching by rule of thumb or imitation is not professional practice as we have conceptualized it.

Professional practice is characterized by reflection, experimentation, and inquiry. It involves having a knowledge base on which to make professional judgments and the skills to implement those decisions as instructional strategies. It is predicated on a system of values and governed by a set of norms. For student teachers to be able to internalize those values and norms and to develop those skills and learn the practices of reflection and research, they must be in a learning environment that is designed to support that process. Practice teaching in a traditional school setting will not be able to provide that environment. Only an environment that itself supports those practices *and* that is committed to the education of teachers can provide the appropriate clinical education for professional teachers.

## Education for Uncertainty

One of the characteristics of the clinical education experience in the professional practice school is a focus on helping the new teacher deal confidently with the uncertainties of the practice. It is often the case that teachers, working in isolation, tend to blame themselves for failures that really are the result of an inadequate knowledge base. They believe they ought to be able to do something or ought to know something that is not really possible. Because teachers have little opportunity to work with colleagues and are not trained in collegial settings, they do not know the extent of others' knowledge and ability and therefore they maintain unrealistic views of what may be possible. Once they understand that they are working with an inadequate knowledge base, however, they need to know that it is possible to function effectively nevertheless. Their lack of opportunity to learn this from mentors and peers is a major inadequacy in their training.

Some medical school experiences that have been studied (Fox, 1957) appear to be designed to make students aware of their own limitations and, at the same time, to take responsibility for their own actions. According to Fox, they come to realize that they cannot know everything there is to know; that not everything they need to know is available; and that they can still function under these limitations. How does this learning come about? The process of education and the curriculum of the clinical experience for third- and fourth-year medical students are designed to have this outcome. Medical students learn that they can function on the basis of incomplete knowledge; and much of the inquiry and experimentation that is done by teaching hospital faculty grow out of this uncertainty. *Students learn that inquiry is a part of professional practice.* Some of the experiences of medical students emphasize for them the limitations of the field. Fox describes the autopsy experience, for example, as central to students' learning for uncertainty. Fox identifies three essential understandings that emerge from that experience: (1) the physicians in charge of the case could not save that patient; (2) death cannot be precisely predicted; and (3) causes of death are messy—they often are not easy to pinpoint. Teachers in training, or in practice, for that matter, have no parallel opportunities to learn that the best knowledge available is often not fully adequate and that colleagues can function competently in spite of that inadequacy.

Medical students learn to cope with uncertainty partly by building as much of a knowledge base as they can. This contributes to the sense of growing competence. They begin to feel that the inadequacy is not personal. Through observations they realize that their peers and their teachers are often uncertain, further helping them to cope with the feeling. In those observations they learn that their teachers cope with that uncertainty directly and that inquiry is a chief way of coping.

*When medical students move to the clinical setting, their chief task is to find an organized way to learn in that setting; "learning in action" is a major part of professional practice.* In the clinical setting students are organized into different kinds of learning groups for different tutorials associated with different clinical experiences. They may work in groups of two, five, or more, depending on the setting and what is to be learned. *The relationship with the teaching faculty becomes very important. Faculty members are the providers of much of what students have to learn. Students listen to them reason out loud.*

In the process of learning to cope with uncertainty, medical students learn some very important principles of professional practice. They learn that inquiry is an important part of that practice; that inquiry and experimentation are the way the professional deals with that uncertainty. The second principle they learn is that learning in a clinical setting is different from classroom learning and is an integral part of professional practice. The third principle learned is that what practitioners know is an important part of what students have to learn; practitioners' knowledge is different from the book learning that has preceded it and accompanies it.

The experience of the intern teacher in a professional practice school must be structured to support these kinds of learning. This requires a whole-school orientation, norms that support collegiality, opportunities for public practice, and some sort of support system for the interns to establish a sense of community among themselves, as well as within the school. Interns must be grouped for different experiences and for a variety of formal instructional experiences. It should be a structured and purposeful program. Professional practice is not learned by osmosis.

### Institutional Requirements for Professional Education

In his discussion of educating the professional, Schön (1987) points out that the fit between this kind of professional education and the traditional university is problematic (pp. 309–310). Whereas the university is grounded in academic theoretical and applied research, reflective practice is grounded in inquiry in action. It requires the knowledge base that the university can provide, but the structure of the university itself and its norms and culture do not support the kind of educational experience implied by the characteristics of reflective practice. On the other hand, a history of successful school/university collaboration does exist in many places. In some important ways, the professional practice schools can be the vehicle that supports this collaboration. In any event, it is important that professional education have its own language, its own traditions, its own systems and expectations, distinct from the academic environment of the university. It needs to develop a structure that models and values public practice, reflection, and collegiality. These are all arguments for the establishment of the professional practice school.

## CHARACTERISTICS OF PROFESSIONAL PRACTICE SCHOOLS

With these assumptions and values at the core of the conversation, the AFT Task Force on Professional Practice Schools began identifying what a professional practice school might look like. What emerged was a set of characteristics that might provide a framework for individual efforts to design such schools. Those characteristics, presented below, were subsequently articulated as standards in a paper prepared for the task force by Holly Houston (1988).

### Support of Student Learning

To fulfill this part of the mission the professional practice school should have certain characteristics.

1. A shared vision of learning among faculty, administration, school board, parents, and students
2. Flexibility in organization of instruction to permit teachers to get to know students well
3. Accountability measures that are appropriate to the goals for student learning
4. Clearly articulated and high standards
5. Management focused on achievement of results rather than delivery of programs
6. Problem-solving and consultation activities that focus on the students' collective and individual needs

### Support of Professional Practice

To support student learning, the professional practice school must be structured in a way that supports professional teaching practice. Certain characteristics would provide evidence of such a commitment, including the following:

1. Collegially developed and agreed-upon standards of professional practice
2. A shared decision-making process on questions of both policy and practice, with ultimate authority for decisions affecting professional practice residing with the faculty
3. Collegiality as a norm, supported by providing time and flexibility in scheduling to encourage frequent and ongoing communication, observation, and feedback among members
4. Joint planning and peer teaching among faculty members
5. Support for creating linkages to university faculty
6. Support for the continuous examination of practice through peer observation, consultation, and evaluation of practice
7. Support of choice by providing the opportunity for individuals to choose to participate, as well as the opportunity to select from those who choose to participate
8. Access to materials and journals to support continuous improvement of practice

These characteristics are not all-inclusive. They are indicators of a commitment toward a goal. They may be altered and others developed as more experience is gained in restructuring schools. They are a starting point.

### Support for the Professional Education of Teachers

The professional practice school is also committed to a high-quality induction program for teachers, built on a professional definition of teaching. This commitment needs to be supported by the organization, staffing, and budget of the institution. Supportive characteristics might include

1. Provision of resources *expressly* for this purpose
2. Provision of time adequately allocated for this purpose
3. Selection of professional practice school staff who demonstrate the skills, attitudes, and knowledge necessary for professional education roles
4. Provision of in-service programs for teaching faculty to support their professional education roles
5. An administrative structure that clearly provides for the management of resources (financial and human) dedicated to this function, including the appointment of a "chief of staff" who is responsible for it
6. Differentiated staffing with full-time faculty and university research

faculty responsible for *both* student education and professional education

7. Adjunct faculty from other schools assigned for specific time periods or acting as adjuncts in their home school to ensure scope and depth of experience for the intern

## Support of Inquiry Directed at the Improvement of Practice

The concept of the school as a center of inquiry for both students and teachers is central to the professional practice school. Students are engaged in active learning; teachers are engaged in inquiry-based practice. The structure, organization, and values of the school support these roles. Interns are there to learn how to be professional practitioners in these school environments. An important function of the professional practice school is to contribute to the knowledge base that supports professional practice. Some of the ways in which it may achieve this goal are

1. Through the establishment of a review board that may include faculty members and outside experts to review research being done in the professional practice school
2. By influencing teacher interns through exposure to the kinds of thinking, problem solving, and inquiry going on in the research of the school faculty; through their involvement directly in that research; by training them to use the research process of reflective inquiry or strategic analysis in their own practice
3. Through the allocation of time devoted to collegial interaction to support the planning, implementation, and evaluation of research
4. Through the allocation of space and resources to support the research function
5. By providing management procedures required by the research function (For example, research in practice may necessitate a different sort of record keeping on student growth and development than that typically employed in a traditional school.)

These characteristics are offered as indicators of what one might look at in evaluating whether a school is indeed moving toward becoming a professional practice school. They are not meant to be definitive, but rather suggestive of those characteristics that would be observable indicators of the values, assumptions, and beliefs underlying the developing institution. In Chapter 6 in this volume, Houston expands on the idea of a framework for developing institutional standards for professional practice schools.

## THE COLLABORATIVE NATURE OF PROFESSIONAL PRACTICE SCHOOLS

Because professional practice schools are conceived to be a link between school restructuring and reform in teacher education, it is natural that these schools should be developed and governed collaboratively by university and school, teacher and professor. In Chapter 7 Neufeld deals at length with the issues raised in inter-institutional collaborations of this sort. Suffice it to say they are many and difficult. Nevertheless, it is apparent that there can be no significant change in schooling without reform in teacher education. Research and experience in teaching and in other professions as well point to the central importance of clinical education of the practitioner. Until now, this experience has been at best idiosyncratic—sometimes excellent, sometimes unproductive. It has never been the major purpose of any of the institutions that had a part of the responsibility for it—not the university, not the school district, and not the state. Professional practice schools give to clinical education the importance it deserves and place responsibility for it in the school site, with professionals, where it belongs. The professional practice school combines the expertise and interest of the university, the district, and the profession in the interests of ensuring professional education for teachers.

## REFERENCES

Amarel, M. (1987). The sources of knowledge for teacher preparation programs: The views of teacher educators. In S. Feiman-Nemser (Ed.), *Teacher education and learning to teach: Proceedings of the first annual NCRTE retreat— June 24–26, 1987* (Conference Series 87-1, pp. 47–56). East Lansing: National Center for Research on Teacher Education, Michigan State University.

Cremin, L. A. (1961). *The transformation of the school. Progressivism in American education, 1876–1957.* New York: Knopf.

Dewey, J. (1974). The relation of theory to practice in education. In R. D. Archambault (Ed.), *John Dewey on education: Selected writings* (pp. 313–338). Chicago: University of Chicago Press. (Original work published 1904)

Duckworth, E. (1986). Teaching as research. *Harvard Educational Review, 56*(4), 481–495.

Duckworth, E. (1987). *"The having of wonderful ideas" and other essays on teaching and learning.* New York: Teachers College Press.

Fox, R. C. (1957). Training for uncertainty. In R. K. Merton, G. G. Reader, & P. L. Kendall (Eds.), *The student-physician. Introductory studies in the sociology of medical education* (pp. 207–241). Cambridge, MA: Harvard University Press.

Houston, H. (1988). *Professional practice schools: How would we know one if we saw one?* Paper commissioned by AFT under a grant from the Exxon Education Foundation.

Kennedy, M. M. (1987). *Inexact sciences: Professional education and the development of expertise* (Issue Paper 87–2). Michigan: National Center for Research on Teacher Education.

Little, J. W. (1982). Norms of collegiality and experimentation: Workplace conditions of school success. *American Educational Research Journal, 19,* 325–340.

Ludmerer, K. (1985). *Learning to heal: The development of American medical education.* New York: Basic Books.

Mitchell, L. S. (1950). *Our children and our schools.* New York: Simon & Schuster.

Perrone, V. (1989). *Working papers: Reflections on teachers, schools, and communities.* New York: Teachers College Press.

Reynolds, M. C. (Ed.). (1989). *Knowledge base for the beginning teacher.* Oxford: Pergamon Press.

Schaefer, R. J. (1967). *The school as a center of inquiry.* New York: Harper & Row.

Schön, D. A. (1983). *The reflective practitioner.* San Francisco: Jossey-Bass.

Schön, D. A. (1987). *Educating the reflective practitioner.* San Francisco: Jossey-Bass.

Shulman, L. S. (1986, February). Those who understand: Knowledge growth in teaching. *Educational Researcher,* pp. 4–14.

Stones, E. (1987). Student (practice) teaching. In M. J. Dunkin (Ed.), *International encyclopedia of teaching and teacher education* (pp. 681–685). New York: Pergamon.

Zeichner, K. M., & Liston, D. P. (1987). Teaching student teachers to reflect. *Harvard Educational Review, 57*(1), 23–48.

# 2 | Child as Meaning Maker: The Organizing Theme for Professional Practice Schools

## ELLEN M. PECHMAN

> What [children's] bodies, minds, and emotions will be like as they are grow-ing and when they are grown depends to an appreciable extent on how they are exercised. ((Mitchell, 1950, p. 9)
>
> Meaning is not given to us in our encounters, but it is given by us—con-structed by us, each in our own way, according to how our understanding is currently organized. (Duckworth, 1987, p. 112)

Professional practice schools are designed to transform the mission of teaching from truth telling and inculcating knowledge (Cohen, 1988) to guiding invention and inquiry (Levine, 1988). This changing vision is inextricably linked to society's transition from an industry- to an infor-mation-driven economy and to a modern conception of children and learning.

Until recently, schools were structured to develop the intellectual po-tential of only a limited segment of society. They successfully educated the highest achievers whose learning needs were a natural match for the narrow range of teaching practices offered. Others who were less intuitive about text-driven and rote learning were dropped or pushed out of schools, destined to find avenues for learning on their own.

Today, rigid school structures and unresponsive teaching continue to discourage too many young people from making a commitment to their education, but this does not have to be the case. Researchers across sev-eral social science disciplines have demonstrated that *all* children are nat-urally motivated to learn. Regardless of circumstance, culture, or prior experience, they are inspired by what Getzels (1977) called "the chal-lenge of the problematic" (p. 495). Learning is active, dynamic, and con-tinuous; and, importantly, it is inherently an individual as well as a social experience (Bruner, 1986). During the elementary years especially, chil-

25

dren are remarkably adaptive and inventive. The challenge for schools is to engage their full capacities in a curriculum that benefits both them and their community.

This perspective on learning is not new; it dates back to Plato. Now, however, solid empirical evidence—drawn from education, psychology, anthropology, and sociology—provides a supportive rationale for framing schools that reflect this view. In addition, new technology and information systems both require and enable the implied changes in teaching. In an age of ready access to computer bulletin boards and conferencing, video displays, interactive television, and other satellite-transmitted information, practitioners can, more easily than ever before, exchange ideas, share their developing procedures, and objectively evaluate their achievements.

The discussion in this chapter establishes the rationale for professional practice schools within a conception of the learner as a "problem-finding" organism (Getzels, 1977, p. 495). It demonstrates how a shifting paradigm of learning alters teaching and schooling. When learning is recognized as the process children use to create meaning out of a vivid collage of events and ideas, schools are designed differently than they have been in the past. Three assumptions about children and their cognitive processes are guiding principles.

1. Children are natural learners (Getzels, 1977; Laboratory of Comparative Human Cognition, 1983), and are always constructing meaning from the culture in which they live.
2. Learning is fundamentally a social and group experience, requiring continual interchange and negotiation among peers and adults (Collins, 1984; Piaget, 1972b, 1973).
3. The purpose of education is to connect children to their culture and community in the widest sense. "The language of education," suggests Bruner (1986), "is the language of culture creating, not of knowledge consuming or knowledge acquisition alone" (p. 133).

This understanding of children and learning combines with advances in modern technology to compel a different kind of teaching. Active, social learners require responsive and inventive learning environments. Professional practice schools, described in the other chapters of this book, are envisioned as such settings both for children and for adults. This chapter concentrates on children, answering three basic questions.

1. Who are the learners to be served by professional practice schools?

2. How do they learn?
3. How should classrooms and schools be organized to meet their needs?

## WHO ARE THE LEARNERS?

Early in the twentieth century, more than 90% of students left high school before graduation (Resnick & Resnick, 1977). Today, national graduation rates are about 75%, but the 25% who do not finish school are disproportionately minorities from low-income families (Levin, 1989). In some areas, especially in cities or remote rural communities, dropout levels exceed 50%.

This loss of human potential is immense, especially given society's capacity to educate its youth. The rapidly changing demography, combined with a modernized view of learning, requires that schools demonstrate better sensitivity about who learners are.

### Demographic Characteristics

America's schools were designed for the Norman Rockwell family: father at work and mother at home with two children. Today only 7% of the country's families fit this description (Hodgkinson, 1988). In the past quarter century, school populations have changed in five major ways.

**Changing family networks.** The role and function of the American family has been transformed by dramatic economic and cultural adjustments. Offices and factories have replaced families and neighborhoods as primary social institutions, undermining the family's responsibility for rearing and socializing its children and leaving children without a reliable social structure for support (Coleman, 1987; see also deLone, 1979). Coleman argues that this phenomenon has eroded critical "social capital"—the norms, social networks, and relationships that motivate children's formal learning and connect them as contributing members to a community (1987, p. 36). As a corporate economy begins to dominate, community connections that bonded earlier generations break down. Families, neighborhoods, and friendships crumble, threatening children's psychological well-being (Coleman, 1987).

When family and community ties to children weaken, it becomes increasingly necessary for government to set policies to counteract disruptive effects of economic and social adjustments. Schools are a significant resource that, if properly planned, could help restore the nurturing and direction children need in a fast-paced technological world. In strengthening schools and other government-sponsored supports, however, parental authority and responsibility for guiding development of their children must be sustained (Zigler, Kagan,& Klugman, 1983).

**Growing proportion of minorities.** More than one-third of the nation's students come from nonwhite, immigrant families segregated from the American mainstream (Ogbu, 1987). Living in cultural isolation within an apparently affluent society, children in these pockets usually learn to function well within their home culture. Unfortunately, the skills and attitudes that are most useful at home often do not generalize well in the broader community (Comer, 1988a).

Schools historically neglected or even rejected many nonmainstream parents, making the families a large "disempowered minority" (Cummins, 1986) for whom schools are alien and uninviting. Minority status, compounded by economic segregation, leaves families understandably skeptical about the value of education. Having failed to make workable connections themselves, many are uncertain about how to help children through a social and economic maze that blocked their own development.

**Relatively more low-income children.** Poverty and economic isolation also separate children from their schools and teachers and constitute another distinctive characteristic of today's student population (Berlin & Sum, 1988). Children represent the largest segment of the nation's poor—almost 25% of all children and 17% of school-age children live in poverty (Hodgkinson, 1988). In all, about 30% of children in schools come from low-income families (Levin, 1988), and the figure is rising rapidly.

Poverty, like culture, is a formidable barrier between families and community services. Typically, low-income communities are served by the worst systems. Insufficient nutrition and health care are likely to be obstacles to children's full development, and schools do a poor job of compensating where other systems fail. As Brandwein (1981) laments, "All things considered, specific communities get the kind of schools their economic and social conditions permit" (p. 3).

**Increasing numbers of students with varying abilities.** Larger proportions of children with wide ability ranges are in mainstream schools (Hodgkinson, 1988). Medical advances make it possible for more low-birthweight, premature, drug-affected, and otherwise fragile babies to survive. But, with poor nutrition and inadequate medical services, there is a 30% chance that their physical or cognitive development is permanently damaged (Hodgkinson, 1988). Moreover, high birth rates among the least affluent and most isolated populations, combined with rapid immigration of child-bearing adults from vastly different societies, increase the number of children who come to school minimally prepared for formal learning.

Schools are potentially the most powerful agency society has to assist children with special cognitive, physical, and emotional needs. Thus, they are rightly charged with serving all children, regardless of physical or emotional abilities or variation in cultural experiences (Kagan, 1989). But, as Kagan notes, schools cannot accomplish this goal without adapting organizational and instructional approaches to accommodate the individual and diverse special needs of students.

**Need of every student to be educated more fully.** A final factor that alters the demographic landscape in schools today is that every child now needs a complete education before entering the job market. Until recently, disaffected students could drop out of school, find a job, and begin at an early age to raise a family. In a technological and information-driven economy, however, there are few jobs for people without an education (Levin, 1989). Today when teenagers begin their families before completing school, they are unable to adequately support themselves or their children.

### Aligning School and Home

Children make the smoothest adjustments to new environments if there are relatively few accommodations for them to make. White and Siegel (1984) explain the problem for children this way.

> It is the somewhat pleasant, but scary, destiny of small children to be faced constantly with the task of going to where they have never been before, of meeting and dealing with people they have never seen before, of doing things they have never done before. In a new environment, they have to arrive at emotional and social settlements before they begin to enter into the problems and processes of intellectual problem solving. They have to ask, "Is it safe here?" "Can somebody like me be here?" "Can I trust the people here?" "Can I trust myself to manage what I have to?" (p. 253)

As a result of the great diversity of cultures, experiences, and basic needs in American society, a closer alignment between home and school is especially necessary when children make their earliest forays away from home. The all-too-frequent "social misalignment" between home and school that is typical in immigrant or minority communities impairs relationships among children, teachers, and families. The resulting mutual mistrust and alienation are difficult to overcome (Comer, 1988a, 1988b).

As Cremin (1966) and others point out, schools alone cannot (nor should they be asked to) make up for all the barriers children face at society's hands. They can, however, create opportunities for children to overcome hurdles. Learning happens best in familiar and secure environments. When classroom experiences and cultures are compatible, children are more likely to make an easy transition (deLone, 1979; Hale, 1982). Schools rooted in the community affirm children's dignity and inculcate a sense of personal identity and commitment. Intense personal involvement, persistence, continuity, and intimacy—these are the elements that bond young people and their society (see Schorr & Schorr, 1988; Zigler, Kagan, & Klugman, 1983).

## HOW DO CHILDREN LEARN?

According to broadened definitions of intelligence, inventiveness and creativity are uniquely human qualities. As natural problem solvers, children spontaneously determine coping strategies in new circumstances, even without direct teaching (Piaget, 1964, 1967; Resnick, 1987b; Sternberg, 1982; Weinberg, 1989). Intelligence encompasses more than what is measured by outmoded IQ and achievement tests (Gardner, 1985; Sternberg & Wagner, 1986). It includes a range of adaptive behaviors and information processing strategies and skills, initially developed in infancy that persist throughout life.

It is only by closely observing learning wherever and however it occurs that researchers will be able to inform teaching practice. Studies of cognitive growth conducted in everyday contexts (Lave, 1988; Rogoff & Lave, 1984) have usefully differentiated cognition—the processes individuals use to acquire knowledge—and school learning, the specific tasks designed to accumulate knowledge about a curriculum (Wagner & Sternberg, 1986).

### New Views of Learning and Intelligence

A "constructivist" view of learning, following Piaget's (1964, 1967, 1972b) ideas about intellectual development, replaces traditional concepts (see also Bruner, 1966). Piaget saw intelligence as actions by individuals that change the way they relate to the world. Research generated by his thinking has led to consensus: "We are in the midst of a major convergence of psychological theories," Resnick (1987a) points out, and "today, cognitive scientists generally share [with Piaget] the assumption that knowledge is constructed by learners" (p. 19).

Knowledge is built from conflict and contradiction, especially when it arises among peers (Frey & Lupart, 1987; Liben, 1987). When children's concepts are inadequate for them to make sense of their experiences, they modify those ideas into something more workable. Thus, children are always posing problems, building solution theories, and testing outcomes, often in collaboration with each other.

Such collaboration provides a "scaffold" for learners to climb (Fischer & Bullock, 1984). It connects children's own thinking with the thinking of others to produce new results and to promote growth. In this way, teachers, parents, friends, and even well-structured teaching tools continue to stimulate children's development and learning (see also Bruner, 1986; Cazden, 1988; Piaget, 1972a, 1973; Vygotsky, 1962). People use this dynamic process to creatively meet the intellectual demands of their lives. It is "mind in action" (Scribner, 1986)—intelligence at work (Wagner & Sternberg, 1986).

Discoveries about complex strategies learners spontaneously use to solve problems have led scientists to identify new ways to assess and describe intelligence and achievement. Traditional measures turned out to be of limited use to understand children's thinking, so cognitive psychologists have begun to examine children's routine decision making to determine how they acquire knowledge and learn to reason. The resulting theories move away from an idea of intelligence as a general trait that can be measured by pencil-and-paper tests. The newer view suggests instead that there are several distinct mental capabilities that are best assessed by performance in context (Resnick & Klopfer, 1989; Weinberg, 1989).

Howard Gardner's theory of "multiple intelligences" (1985; Walters & Gardner, 1986) is the most recent example of this thinking. Gardner and his colleagues identify seven intelligences and examples of how they are applied.

1. Musical (composers, performers, sophisticated musical listeners)
2. Bodily kinesthetic (athletes, dancers, actors, crafters)
3. Logical-mathematical (scientists, mathematicians, logicians)
4. Linguistic (poets, orators, writers)
5. Spatial (navigators, geometers, sculptors, artists, surgeons)
6. Interpersonal (knowledge of other persons typical of politicians, teachers, therapists)
7. Intrapersonal (orientation toward one's feelings and emotions)

Each intelligence follows a different developmental path, typically peaks at varying ages, and calls for specific kinds of encouragement. These facilities and skills permit people to resolve genuine difficulties, create socially valued products, or lay the groundwork for new knowledge (for example, create a story, make a kite, or anticipate a move in chess). Any given intelligence simultaneously relies on several faculties and dimensions. Thus, Gardner notes that dance uses bodily and kinesthetic skills, as well as varying degrees of musical, interpersonal, and spatial intelligence. Because human roles require several intelligences, individuals develop collections of aptitudes rather than singular abilities.

Individuals differ in the profiles of intelligence they exhibit in a particular context (Gardner, 1991). Moreover, they may not be gifted in any single intelligence, but may have a combination of skills that enables them to contribute uniquely to specific situations. Gardner argues that in a complex and diverse society, all people, properly guided, nurtured, and encouraged, develop clusters of abilities so they can make original contributions.

A second recent approach to studying intelligence is called information processing, a step-by-step analysis that describes how people gather information and knowledge (Siegler, 1986). Thinking mechanisms, considered to be universal, are believed to develop with maturity, experience, and training. Examples are learning from experience and selecting and applying appropriate strategies to new situations (Frey & Lupart, 1987; Liben, 1987).

Finally, Ceci and Liker (1986) describe a "contextual account of intelligence" (p. 138), best indicated by how people cope with environmental challenges. Their research has shown that

> Each of us possesses innate potentialities for achievement in abstract reasoning, verbal analysis, creative expression, quantification, visual-spatial organization, and so on. . . . Additionally, each of us is exposed to multiple contexts for expressing [our] potentialities. In the types of environments that are typically seen as "enriched," there are opportunities to develop most or even all of one's potentialities. For most, however, the opportunities that are relevant for the actualization of even a single potentiality may not have been available during critical periods of development. (p. 139)

### Practical vs. Academic Intelligence

Scribner (1986) and Wagner and Sternberg (1986) contrast practical thinking and intelligence that characterize day-to-day activities with the academic or formal thinking usually done in school. Practical intelligence uses an array of abilities and flexible thinking styles that may be unrelated or even antithetical to academic performance (Brown, Collins, & Duguid, 1989; Rogoff & Lave, 1984). Adaptive functioning at home, in school, or in the marketplace reflects the capacity to use resources in the environment to learn. Invention, creativity, and the ability to integrate information are working examples of practical intelligence.

Academic intelligence, in contrast, is a formal response to problems posed in classrooms, on examinations, or in a psychologist's office (Ceci & Liker, 1986). Neisser (1976) and Wagner and Sternberg (1986) characterize tasks requiring academic intelligence as follows:

- They are devised by someone other than the learner.
- They often have little or no intrinsic interest to the learner.
- All of the information needed is usually provided.
- Tasks are separated from learners' everyday experiences.
- The tasks usually assume a well-defined and preset correct answer.
- There is a limited number, usually one, of correct methods to find the solution.
- Tasks are presented in written symbols, using words or numbers.

With circumscribed assignments such as these, schools try to teach children to use the formal tools of academic disciplines—vocabulary, mathematical formulas, dictionaries, scientific procedures—but many children find few opportunities outside of school to practice what they are taught. The resulting inauthenticity of classroom activity makes it difficult for children to see how school learning applies to their lives (Brown, Collins, & Duguid, 1989).

Another limitation of many school tasks is that relatively few learners are expected to reach the highest achievement levels. Grading on a curve and tracking students into fixed achievement groups are antiquated customs that assume that most of the curriculum will be mastered by only a few students. Practical thinking and coping skills, on the other hand, have no upper limits. When, for example, children want to meet friends, access a forbidden cabinet, or obtain assistance in an emergency, they can analyze the task, devise a plan, and put their plan into motion.

Some children are more successful at practical thinking than at their school assignments because the context is familiar and they are motivated to succeed (Lepper, 1989). Researchers are rapidly accumulating evidence that this kind of intelligence can be productively directed into various cognitive activities. The challenge for schools is to help children find the connections between their working intelligence and the curriculum so that they build on and use their most practiced capacities both in school and out.

Schools typically employ a narrow range of procedures to assess learning. As a result, highly valued abilities—spontaneous organizing and planning, logical analysis, negotiation, and collaboration—are neither measured nor validated in school. Although these achievements are increasingly essential to society, they are not well developed among children (Presseisen, 1987). As a result, the archaic notion of intelligence as an absolute function is being challenged by a social and contextual definition (Goodnow, 1986) that changes which children are considered the "brightest" and who will function most successfully outside of the classroom.

## Engaging Children's Intelligence in School

Outside of school, children and adults alike pit their ideas against new information and experiences, constantly building on what they already know. Nothing could be more practical; unfortunately, nothing could be less like school lessons, either. When teachers concentrate on understanding how children use their practical intelligence, the teachers can help link the familiar as well as the unexplored, teaching students to apply what they know to academic tasks.

The teacher's role is to encourage students to confront their naive theories, demonstrate how to analyze flaws in their thinking, and help build new knowledge structures. Teaching and learning are rewarding intellectual challenges when viewed in this framework. Teachers are no longer mere disseminators of information; they are instead guides and mentors.

Good examples of this kind of teaching abound. In all the basic school content areas—English, social studies, sciences, and mathematics—significant new thinking shifts away from direct instruction toward active, inventive instruction (Association for Supervision and Curriculum Development, 1990b). The National Council of Teachers of Mathematics (1989) and the American Association for the Advancement of Science (AAAS) are two professional organizations that have taken an especially strong stand to advocate such teaching. The AAAS (1989) summarizes the rationale for a different kind of teaching this way.

> People have to construct their own meaning regardless of how clearly teachers or books tell them things. Mostly, a person does this by connecting new information and concepts to what he or she already believes. Concepts, the essential units of human thought, that do not have multiple links with how

a student thinks about the world are not likely to be remembered or useful. (p. 145)

## Children's Developmental Characteristics

Educational programs that facilitate children's ability to prosper within a changing world are grounded in ever-advancing knowledge about human development. Examples of pedagogical responsiveness are described here in an overview of cognitive and social growth during the elementary and middle-school years. Table 2.1 summarizes major changes in the biological, cognitive, and social domains that occur during these years.

**The primary years.** When children enter kindergarten, around age 5, their cognitive capacities are complex, but logical structures are still being formed. Development depends on concrete physical experiences, vigorous social exchanges about real problems, and thoughtful adult guidance.

Between the ages of 4 and 7, children are inquisitive and yearn to become part of a group. The time is ripe to foster responsibility. Children become more goal directed and more fully involved in family and community life. They can care for themselves, follow simple instructions, gather and use tools for work or play, make decisions, plan, engage in organized play, and profit from formal instruction.

Interpersonal communication, the starting point for building social relationships, is of particular interest. Children are gradually learning to understand others' perspectives. They can make sounder judgments, more accurately distinguish between appearances and reality, and construct and follow logical rules.

As a result of these attainments, peer culture begins to be increasingly influential in the primary years, and learning is most effective when social interaction is valued. Children are fascinated by language and stories. Given the opportunity, they spontaneously and unabashedly dramatize their fantasies and play out evolving world views. They also write creatively when permitted to express themselves freely.

From a young age, children establish an intuitively logical sense of numbers, patterns, and arithmetic relationships. As they work out their own rules and theories about numbers, however, their mathematical logic may contain flaws that need to be "debugged" and "repaired" (Resnick & Ford, 1981). This connection is accomplished through guided experimentation and construction that replaces "buggy rules" with more reliable and accurate ones.

Parents exert the strongest influence on young children's lives, and

**Table 2.1  Distinctive features of biological, cognitive, and social development**

| *Early Childhood*<br>*Ages 4-7* | *Midle Childhood*<br>*Ages 8-10* | *Early Adolescence*<br>*Ages 11-15* |
|---|---|---|
| *Biological Domain* | | |
| • Brain size increases<br>• Waking and sleeping periods change<br>• Large and small muscle coordination increases<br>• Child gains greater control over body, taking on more complex physical tasks | • Physical size and activity increase<br>• Agility and fine muscle coordination improves<br>• Brain matures, supporting subtle and complex thought and problem solving<br>• Permanent teeth come in | • Primary and secondary sexual characteristics develop<br>• Physical size and shape increase, creating adult-like appearance<br>• Adolescent reaches 98% of adult height by end of growth spurt |
| *Cognitive Domain* | | |
| • Child learns to use linguistic and numerical symbol systems<br>• Manipulate concrete objects for intellectual exploration<br>• Use real events to stabilize uneven operational thought<br>• Categorize and organize, improving memory strategies<br>• Invent rules spontaneously to guide thought and action | • Concrete experiences remain the basis for learning<br>• Memory capacity and use of strategic remembering increase<br>• Organized thinking improves<br>• Concrete operational thought develops logical precision with quantitative problems | • Mature thinking processes and the ability to conceptualize develop<br>• Formal operations aid the ability to abstract beyond the present<br>• Adolescent thinks about self in the social world and begins to assess own ability to perform against that of others<br>• Values are increasingly affected by the interaction of gender and culture |
| *Social Domain* | | |
| • Child better understands others' points of view<br>• Thinks more clearly about how others see his or her ideas and actions<br>• Plays with words and thoughts<br>• Shares and dramatizes stories and community lore<br>• Demonstrates that fantasy, dramatic play, and egocentrism are still very important in all aspects of development | • Child participates actively with peer group<br>• Plays games with defined rules and rituals<br>• Is increasingly responsive to deliberate instruction<br>• Adheres to rules as absolute<br>• Allows parents and teachers to structure and guide actions<br>• Compares self to others | • Desire for autonomy and search for identity and sense of competences increase<br>• Adolescent begins to take moral and political stands<br>• Peers become more central<br>• Strong identity with and need for family continue as awareness of sex, sexuality, and demands of the peer group increase |

*Sources:* Adelson, 1986; Almy, 1975; Almy, Chittenden, & Miller, 1966; Biber, 1984; Bredekamp, 1987; Cohen, 1972; Cole & Cole, 1989; Collins, 1984; Eccles & Midgley, 1988; Elkind, 1974; Flavell & Markman, 1983; Katz, 1977; Lipsitz, 1984; Paley, 1984; Piaget, 1967; Simmons & Blyth, 1987; White & Siegel, 1984

cultures and their communities offer more or less structured guidance. In the United States, for example, preschools were long the luxury of a small wealthy elite. Changing work and family patterns, however, have created such gaps in resources available to children that policy makers now consider day-long schools and after-school care basic social needs that are shared by children in every sector of society (Hamburg, 1987; Shanker, 1987; Zigler, 1987).

**The middle childhood years.** The years from 8 to 10 aptly have been called the "age of industry" (Erikson, 1950). Children have a keen interest in objects and ideas and become intensely involved in their surroundings. Language is well developed for social use. During these years of vigorous physical growth, children readily test their developing strength in imaginative, spontaneous play.

Social growth, including sexual and ethnic identity, deepens during the middle years, and peer groups become even more important. Children are fascinated with rules—moral rules, social conventions, and personal codes. They often challenge adult authority, and they are sticklers for fairness. Friendships emphasize shared interests, mutual understanding, and trust. Developing abilities to adopt others' points of view and to debate lead children to take friendships increasingly seriously.

Cognitive skills expand during these years and become more abstract and logically elaborate. After age 8, children are usually quite receptive to learning more substantive information, although they still learn best through experimentation. Moreover, awareness of the community broadens, and they become eager to examine issues such as the environment or health. Until about age 10, children still have difficulty with concepts not based on personal experience. They begin to combine, separate, reorder, and transform objects and ideas in their minds, and they develop these skills earlier and faster in physical than social sciences (Cohen, 1972). Their curiosity is nurtured when they grapple with increasingly complex information that is emotionally powerful and conceptually appropriate. Well-planned schools, those that provide an active curriculum that integrates the content areas, are a potent social and intellectual influence during middle childhood.

**Early adolescence.** The social and moral fabric of school becomes an especially important contributor to development from 11 to 15, when youngsters' experiences coalesce into an integrated identity. Beliefs, abilities, and desires are—or are not—reconciled with community norms. "Education for a well-spent youth" is how James (1972) describes society's obligation to young adolescents, but how to accomplish this in an uncertain world is especially puzzling.

This search for personal value is in step with the predictably unpredictable physical changes that accompany the onset of puberty. For girls, rapid growth starts as early as 10½, usually followed by menarche at about 12. For boys, the spurt begins about a year later than for girls and peaks at about 14 (Tanner, 1978, 1987). During this period, children are able to become parents, so accurate information must be offered with warm, realistic guidance. The social, emotional, and intellectual metamorphoses that coincide with these physical changes make this time a very perplexing one for children and adults. Family remains the most compelling force, even when interactions with parents are strained (Adelson, 1986; Steinberg, 1989).

The ages between 10 and 15 were once considered a time of abnormal tumult. We now know they are continuous with other periods of growth (Elkind, 1974). The search for gender identity, combined with eagerness for independence, encourages young adolescents to seek stronger bonds with peers. Risk taking during these years approximately parallels that of the general adult population (Offer, Ostrov, & Howard, 1981). Adults who work with young adolescents must channel this dynamic energy into activities that develop a mature attachment to home and community.

Cognitive advances of this period open a panorama of opportunities to build new connections among young adolescents and the adult world. Gradually, through experience, young adolescents learn to juggle multiple alternatives, scrutinize their thoughts, look beyond immediate limitations, and hypothesize options. Teens' thought processes are more mature, but direct experiences continue to be necessary grist for the intellectual mill. Demonstrations of concrete solutions to hypothetical problems make it possible for young adolescents to comprehend more abstract and logical thought. Thus, responsive classrooms encourage debate, discussion, and group interaction. They employ interactive technology and scientific experimentation, as well as traditional reading, writing, and problem solving.

Programs for young adolescents must be intrinsically interesting, involving them in projects that inspire connections to peers, learning, and community. Schools nurture maturity by promoting work in small teams of students and adults and by valuing autonomy and creativity (Lipsitz, 1984). It is no longer possible to "induct young people into agreed-upon certainties," warns James (1972). At this age "we have to coopt them into uncertainty" (p. 43). Young people who grapple with the unknown learn to recognize that factual knowledge is fleeting, and, in doing so, they become prepared to face what lies ahead.

## Developmental Continuity

Despite their different capacities, all children share the same fundamental psychoeducational needs.

- *Psychological safety*—Emotional security developed from self-understanding
- *Esteem and self-worth*—A realistic self-perception acquired through significant success and connections to family, community, and peers
- *Connectedness with adults and peers*—Sustained relationships that bind children to the people around them
- *Caring guidance*—Authoritative, encouraging, and structured support that enables children to explore the unknown
- *Intellectual competence and achievement*—Opportunities that empower children to test developing intellectual strengths and experience cognitive, social, and artistic achievements
- *Applied and varied learning experiences*—Meaningful activities through which children can explore the limits of their curiosity and creativity
- *Role models and values*—Adults and peers who unswervingly affirm a community's moral values and encourage children to make similar commitments

An expanded list of psychoeducational needs appears in Table 2.2.

The educational program implied by these factors is perhaps best described by Biber (1984) and her colleagues at Bank Street College as "developmental" and "interactionist" (p. 65). The developmental component emphasizes children's emerging patterns of intellectual, social, emotional, and physical growth. Interaction has two dimensions. The first is an exchange between children and their environments, including adults, other children, and the material world—the content-specific "stuff" of learning. The second is the interaction between cognitive and affective aspects of self.

A developmental and interactionist education attends to the collaboration and co-learning between child and setting (Fischer & Bullock, 1984). Structured to respond to the full range of children's needs, it aims to establish continuity for learning between home and school.

Finally, developmentally responsive schools must accommodate three other critical aspects of learning: (1) the whole child—artistic dimensions, feelings, uniqueness, and cultural variations; (2) the intricate ways children are motivated; and (3) the different routes by which they develop a conscience that evolves into a system of ethics. This list is de-

**Table 2.2  Children's psychoeducational needs**

| Early Childhood<br>Ages 4-7 | Midle Childhood<br>Ages 8-10 | Early Adolescence<br>Ages 11-15 |
|---|---|---|
| *Psychological Safety* | | |
| Deep sense of personal and emotional safety, psychological connectedness, and trust | Positive feelings toward self and a sense of personal mastery | Safe environment to explore autonomy and identity issues and to develop understanding of multiple changes that are occurring |
| *Esteem and Self-Worth* | | |
| Adequate self-esteem, measured against criteria established by home, family, community, and ethnic group | Realistic perception of self and others in terms of life circumstances; flexible group alignments and strong friendships | Meaningful opportunities to develop competence and achievement through participation in the community |
| *Connectedness to Adults and Peers* | | |
| Child and adult models who exemplify and help children develop qualities the community values | Relatedness and ability to develop deep and warm connections | Opportunities to explore and define identity and discover talents in collaboration with same- and opposite-gender adults and peers |
| *Caring Guidance* | | |
| Authoritative and clear direction from caring and responsive adults | Relatedness and connectedness to the community; experiences to develop capacities and responsibilities in new contexts | Structured and well-defined limits developed and enforced jointly by adults and peers |
| *Intellectual Competence and Achievement* | | |
| Adults and peers to help deepen, construct, and make sense of the child's many worlds against real-life contexts | Opportunities for open and independent thinking, combined with encouragement to seek and accept assistance in new content domains | Experiences that test and extend cognitive capacity for abstract thinking through a multiplicity of activities, experiences, and relationships |
| *Applied and Varied Learning Experiences* | | |
| Experiences that are inherently satisfying, interesting, and authentic, constructed by children on the basis of their own conception of the world | Connections that develop curiosity and creativity by expanding and reorganizing knowledge, especially in science and the arts | Physical and social activity through which to define & explore experiences associated with physical, social, emotional, and intellectual changes |
| *Role Models and Values* | | |
| Relationships with adults who are clear and confident about their values and work with children toward those values | Opportunities to build coping strength and to gain equilibrium in the face of challenges and obstacles | Affirming interactions with adult & peer role models who represent community moral values; experience with others exploring ways to achieve agreed-upon ethical standards |

*Sources:* Early childhood—Bredekamp, 1987; Katz, 1977; Middle childhood—Cohen, 1972; Elkind, 1974; Early adolescence—Eccles & Midgley, 1988; Lipsitz, 1984

manding, but the process of human development is complex. All these elements are essential to understanding learners and must therefore be cornerstones of schools that nurture children's meaning making.

## IMPLICATIONS FOR SCHOOLS

By the time children begin school, they are experienced thinkers who craft knowledge from the interplay between their experiences and their growing capacity for self-aware, goal-directed thought (Belmont, 1989; Linney & Seidman, 1989). Development is strongly influenced by family history, ethnicity, language, and socioeconomic factors. Although children's backgrounds may affect their reactions to school learning, their differences are fundamentally rooted in practical knowledge and situations, both of which are highly malleable in school-age children (deLone, 1979).

### Responsibilities in a Culturally Diverse Society

Schools that respond sensitively to children's diversity support them and the community. Successful teachers affirm students' individuality by analyzing what children already know and then embedding instruction in the familiar. Families are valued as true educational partners who can provide insights about children's learning styles and interests. Four areas of family–school collaboration have been identified by the Laboratory of Comparative Human Cognition (1983).

- Provide specific information children need to understand and feel comfortable with each new experience
- Present information in familiar ways until children learn to use it to further their independent learning
- Connect home, school, and community so children become personally involved in each and satisfied that they belong
- Structure the difficulty level of learning so information is accessible

To these, Linney and Seidman (1989) add two others.

- Avoid labeling children, focusing instead on interactions that promote learning
- Support the whole child's social, emotional, and cognitive growth

When cultural diversity is genuinely respected, educators adapt to students' idiosyncratic responses and accommodate the community's languages and circumstances. School programs that adjust to students greatly enhance the quality of education for all.

## Classrooms That Mediate Learning

Mature, effective learners are self-aware and capable of deliberately using goal-oriented strategies (Bransford, Vye, Adams, & Perfetto, 1989). Children develop this maturity by working with teachers who relinquish their outmoded role as dispensers of knowledge and instead focus on how students think and on how knowledge develops. These teachers—learning mediators—help students connect their experiences and cognitive strategies to curriculum content.[1]

This approach stimulates thinking and simultaneously helps students create meanings from content. Figure 2.1 depicts the flow of exchange between student and curriculum through the teacher. When teachers skillfully mediate between learners and curriculum, they diagnose, facilitate, model, motivate, and guide. They encourage students to broaden their "courage spans," so they can accept failure as a temporary false start, and to inspect errors for useful information (Brown, 1989). By showing children how to analyze their learning, teachers instill self-motivation toward mastery (Ames & Archer, 1988). They inspire children to "mess about" (Hawkins, 1970, p. 38) and to explore the "having of wonderful ideas" (Duckworth, 1987).

**Figure 2.1 Role of the teacher as mediator**

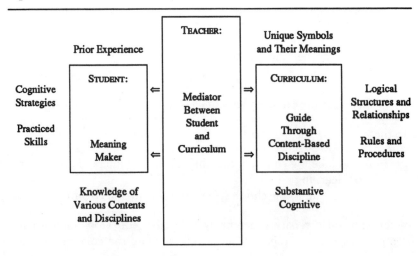

Learners spontaneously attribute their own meanings (born from experience) to symbols and relationships; it is up to teachers to ensure that students' interpretations are consistent with principles of formal disciplines (Resnick & Klopfer, 1989). Children are encouraged to set goals and are given wide latitude about how to get there. This process is not free-floating, however, because the teacher puts students in contact with a topic, and then observes and records what is new and interesting. While students explain the sense they make from their new intellectual encounters, the teacher listens attentively, seeking to understand the meanings students construct.

Lampert (1985, 1989) describes a process that helps children connect their naive theories with formal mathematics. Students begin, often with partners or in a group, to figure out how to represent numbers and mathematical operations with familiar words, diagrams, or symbols. Afterward, they write about and discuss their findings. Next, children learn how to select appropriate mathematical ideas to compare alternative solutions and derive results. Their knowledge is then solidified by applying these tools in similar situations and, later, to novel mathematical problems.

Using concrete objects, students adapt understandings of mathematical concepts to problems they invent. Through trial and error, they learn to test conjectures and, through their own constructions, fix emerging concepts and knowledge. As they develop arguments for how they reach solutions, children engage both the logic and content of the discipline. Lampert further strengthens and tests ownership of knowledge by encouraging students to challenge each other's ideas, expecting challengers to demonstrate well-structured mathematical thinking with persuasive evidence.

This reason-based teaching and learning contrasts with authority-based, direct instruction that characterizes most classrooms. First, students explore real mathematical problems with a multitude of meaningful applications and representations. Second, students are involved in a social process—among and between students and teachers—that contributes to expanding ideas they create. Discourse-centered learning involves children as doers and thinkers. "The task," summarizes Glaser (1984), "is to produce a changed environment for learning—an environment in which there is a new relationship between students and their subject matter. . . . As individuals acquire knowledge, they also should be empowered to think and reason" (p. 103).

When education is driven by student inquiry, teachers' methods are interactive and diverse. Students use both oral and written language to explain, describe, elaborate, and defend their evolving knowledge (Cazden, 1988). They learn through many methods, modalities, styles, and technologies (Siegler, 1986) both in and out of school. Reciprocal instruction (Palinscar & Brown, 1984), where teachers and learners exchange roles, reinforces learning by beginning with specific direction and gradually moving to independence (Bransford et al., 1989). Most important, cooperative activities such as groups, games, planning teams, and project work encourage co-learning, analytical processes, decision making, and problem solving (Slavin, 1989; see also Presseisen, 1987). Figure 2.2 depicts the relationship between interactive strategies and learning outcomes that are mediated by students' thinking, elaboration, and analysis.

By opening up new areas of content for students to explore, schools

**Figure 2.2  Connecting teaching strategies with learning outcomes**

## Interactive Teaching Strategies

- Group problem solving
- Decision making
- Reciprocal teaching
- Co-learning
- Peer tutoring
- Collaborative planning
- Project work with real consequences
- Experience with diverse technologies

## Require Students to

- Invent and create
- Explain and describe
- Elaborate and extend
- Defend one's position and knowledge

## Lead Students to

- Analyze and practice through performance
- Integrate ideas
- Expand knowledge
- Evaluate positions and ideas

## Learning Outcomes

- Knowledge and skills contextualized through meaningful experiences
- Active engagement as learners and knowers
- Learners' ownership of knowledge fostered
- Rewards provided through personal connections developed between co-learners and teachers

mold and expand intellectual development while achieving valued social goals. The long-term objective of teaching is to strengthen learners' capacities to think and create. This is not a laissez-faire approach, nor does it give children exclusive control over what or how they learn. Instead, responsibility for learning results from interactions between child and environment that the teacher thoughtfully and skillfully shapes.[2]

The outcomes of inquiry-driven instruction are portfolios of student work (ASCD, 1990a). Standardized and group tests have a place, but only to reflect broadly on average accomplishments of grades, schools, or districts. Individual progress is measured by the student's practical facility with subject material. The intrinsic value of learning is rewarded through personal connections among students and teachers. The "products" are the children's abilities to apply knowledge and their accompanying sense of competence.

**Diagnostic teaching.** Diagnosis is a strategy for identifying and teaching within a child's "zone of proximal development," the appropriate level between the lowest point of achievement where the child works independently and the upper limit at which the child learns in collaboration with the teacher (Vygotsky, 1962; Wertsch, 1985). Responsibility for performance and practice is the child's, with the impetus of progressive explanations, hints, and encouragement from the teacher. Teachers' queries enable children to reconstruct and verify knowledge until they can apply it. Diagnostic teachers analyze and design experiences, suggestions, and demonstrations that gradually move children along (Leinhardt, 1989).

The art of this diagnostic process is to strike a subtle balance between waiting for students to become aware of the possibilities and actively stimulating learning. Even when adults provide explicit clues, the collaboration itself instills faith that it is vital for children to continue to invest in learning (Brown, Bransford, Ferrara, & Campione, 1983). This teaching process is neither objective-based nor book-learned. It develops from reflective teaching, undertaken by teacher-researchers who craft workable pedagogies that respond expertly to children's evolving understanding of their world (Duckworth, 1987).

**Language development.** Children's interactions and thinking styles are formed by their oral language. Through language, communities transmit rules, behavioral expectations, and values. When school language is consistent with that used at home, children make connections. By contrast, when the home vernacular differs from the teacher's, the communication barriers can be formidable (Cazden, 1988; Heath, 1989).

Language development in school begins informally through conversations that introduce learners and teachers. Communication flows smoothly when schools deliberately plan to collaborate with children and their families, especially when cultural differences exist (Cazden, 1988). Mastery of school language is often an essential first step toward building understanding and trust. Similarly, when teachers use the families' languages, they gain a perspective that enables them to teach from their students' vantage points.

**Alternative classroom organizational structures.** Manipulating classroom organization while holding class size constant is one effective approach to improving the quality of interactions between students and teachers. There are many ways this can be accomplished. Class size can be adjusted for specific activities and lessons by having paraprofessionals, volunteers, and older students lead working groups and mentor students in various contexts. Cooperative and peer-directed lessons also promote problem solving and high levels of cognitive response (Slavin, 1989; Slavin & Madden, 1989).

Research consistently demonstrates that didactic instruction has little value unless it accommodates diversity (Cole, Griffin, & the Laboratory of Comparative Human Cognition, 1987; Slavin, 1989). Every class, even if clustered by ability, includes students with a range of skills. Thus, teachers must adapt flexible, variably paced lessons that incorporate technology, real-life problems, and materials. Only when instruction is adjusted for students' individuality, and provides opportunities for student interaction, are teacher-directed lessons optimally effective (Meece, Blumenfeld, & Puro, 1989; Stodolsky, 1988).

Adoption of alternative school structures is increasingly widespread. Gardner (1991) advocates a mix of techniques that concurrently engage students' developing strengths. In "flow centers" students tackle problems of personal interest. An apprentice system brings together children of different ages to work on special interests or skills. "Domain projects" teach concepts and skills in art forms such as rehearsing music or writing plays. Each project simultaneously stresses production and calls for reflection and analysis en route to the performance.

Versions of these strategies are used in schools seeking more intimate learning settings. Examples include elementary schools influenced by the Harvard-based research group Project Zero (Blythe & Gardner, 1990), the comprehensive schools in Germany (AFT Staff, 1988), and American middle (Lipsitz, 1984) and high schools (Coalition of Essential Schools, 1985; Oxley, 1989).

Gardner (1991) also believes that effective schools structure education around several "cycles of emphasis." The initial years, for example, might foster creativity through free choice. The first formal education, after the age of 8, would focus on skills and knowledge in a common curriculum. From high school through the undergraduate years, electives and cross-disciplinary courses would have several formats. A period of professional training would round out one's education, allowing the fullest probe of options before choosing a career.

Classroom organization is pivotal in determining the quality of learning. Research in this area has generated a range of theories that are being examined (Slavin, 1989). No single approach or set of approaches emerges as appropriate in all settings; however, alternative grouping practices consistently increase the amount and quality of time devoted to learning.

**Thinking skills.** Cognitive psychologists who study learning efficiency argue that metacognitive strategies—those directed at helping students analyze their own thought processes—can be taught (Bransford et al., 1989; Frey & Lupart, 1987; Siegler, 1986). Although some people learn, remember, and think more effectively than others, this variability rests on prior experience, not on native talent. Two common barriers to effective use of such strategies are a lack of general knowledge about how to analyze and apply information in a specific content area, and an inability to activate thinking or language skills when needed.

Training procedures to improve learners' use of information (Bransford et al., 1989; Perkins, 1986; Perkins & Simmons, 1988; Presseisen, 1987) involve providing students with tools to efficiently acquire new information and analyze their own success. Transferability and application rely on knowledge of the content in which these tools are to be used (Alexander & Judy, 1988; Eylon & Lynn, 1988). Thus, individuals with an inadequate knowledge base are inefficient users of their information-processing strategies. Inquiry teaching and strategy building clearly are most beneficial when they are applied within subject areas.

**The role of technology.** Interactive computer, video, and telecommunications technology are relatively new instructional tools with vast potential, but they are poorly understood and too infrequently tapped (see Cole et al., 1987; Educational Technology Center, 1985; Lepper & Gurtner, 1989). Schools are reluctant to invest in technology because it is expensive, and often early versions are quickly rendered obsolete. Limited training is available to help teachers and curriculum experts learn how to integrate technology within their educational programs. Schools are inherently conservative, too, believing that students must

learn traditional content before they advance to modern modes of thinking or new material, despite evidence that computers promote complex
thinking and coordinate advanced multilevel problem solving (Cole et al.,
1987).

These barriers are particularly unfortunate because technology can
dramatically shift how classrooms and schools are organized. New technologies such as computers and video cameras, united with older technologies such as television, can be used together creatively to alter what
is considered basic in school learning. The challenge is to select technology that advances students' development and thinking without disrupting
workable teaching and learning systems and without further disenfran-
chising any segment of America's diverse society.

## Schools as Centers of Continuity

Research drawn from various academic fields about the nature of learning suggests that schools must expand their role in students' and communities' intellectual and social lives. In addition to being centers of inquiry for children, schools promote learning best when they also link
communities together, functioning as centers of continuity. In tandem
with parents and neighbors, schools have the potential to reroot the erod-
ing social capital and re-establish interconnections among individuals,
families, and groups (Levin, 1988; Schorr & Schorr, 1988). Active learning environments for children are also vibrant learning centers for adults
who connect with one another and with the broader community not only
to support children but also to enhance their own development. Important, too, is the school's commitment to model learning and inquiry processes so parents can use them to encourage their children's connection to
formal learning.

Schools become centers of continuity by including parents as partners in learning and teaching. Families are involved in educational planning, and they are informed about why new programs may look different
from those in other schools or from their own past experiences. Their
comments and interests are solicited, and they have meaningful roles as
program organizers, interpreters, tutors, and advocates. When parents
are involved in school, they know that their children are indeed learning.

For all these reasons, now more than ever, schools need to become
centers—of community, continuity, and inquiry—for students and teachers. Professional practice schools are designed to be such institutions and
to educate teachers to work in them.

## INSTITUTIONALIZING LEARNER-CENTERED INSTRUCTIONAL PRACTICE

The renewed national interest in designing schools that inspire inquiry-centered, active learning has encouraged new model programs. These schools attempt to avoid the pitfalls that stymied similar efforts during the 1960s and early 1970s (see Perrone, 1989).

### Learner-Centered Schools

The most prominent programs, still in their early stages, are spearheaded by researchers implementing theoretical models based on new understandings about cognition. Teams of university faculty and teachers are gradually expanding successful laboratory or ideal school settings.[3] These educationally responsive schools share many common features.

- Learners are viewed as active constructors of meaning. Students use their thinking skills to tackle practical problems, and learning is personalized.
- Assessment is a school-wide process that involves teachers, students, and community. A range of procedures are routinely used to evaluate students' progress, teachers' instruction, and the effects of the program (ASCD, 1990a). New means are sought to evaluate achievement. Typically, samples of student work are collected in portfolios, displays, or manuscripts, instead of using traditional tests.
- Students collaborate, in mixed-age groups and teams, to develop logical thinking and analytical facility through projects of interest. Learning groups are fluid, small, and personal. Community visitors, experts, parents, novice teachers, and peers serve as teachers, tutors, and assistants in learning.
- Course material is uncovered rather than "covered" through an interdisciplinary curriculum. Learners study central concepts in depth, rather than superficially examining ideas and memorizing facts.
- Teachers function as guides and models who demonstrate inquiring attitudes toward knowledge and learning. They avoid serving as the major source of information.
- Recognized as professionals and experts, teachers are fully responsible for determining an appropriate program for students. They are skilled diagnosticians, analysts, and researchers who also involve novice teachers in their work to ensure the continued development of a cadre of future professionals.
- Home and community are connected to schools in significant ways. Be-

cause learning occurs inside as well as outside the school, communities and families are integrated in the children's education.
• Learner-centered programs are found in inner-city systems with children typically considered at risk to fail or drop out.

## Dilemmas

Evaluations from earlier generations of inquiry-centered programs showed several beneficial effects, especially in mathematics, science, and social studies (Kyle, 1984; Minuchin, Biber, Shapiro, & Zimiles, 1969; Winsor, 1973). The active hands-on curricula engaged students in high levels of critical and analytical thinking, improved problem-solving skills, enhanced performance in other content areas, and strengthened social and communications skills. Many teachers welcomed these successful curricula, especially because they were enthusiastically received by students. However, controversy about outcomes, coupled with heavy time demands on administrators and teachers, forced schools to abandon their efforts.

New model programs should not meet such an ignoble end. District- and school-level administrators must protect teachers' energy by scheduling paid collaboration and planning time within the work day so teachers have the opportunity to confront and resolve the tough teaching challenges. Such time allows teachers to tap reservoirs of creative energy otherwise dissipated in the stress of overwork. Properly nurtured, analytical teaching sustains a community-wide commitment to learning.

The dilemma of overcommitting a small group of active and caring educators has taken its toll on all too many great educational programs. Professional practice schools must be created slowly, soundly, and with support, or else goals should be modified and the programs postponed. Schools need the proper institutional structures—professional organizations; teacher education institutions; and state, local, and school levels— to connect them to resources that sustain inquiry-centered learning (Levine, 1988). When united in purpose, commitments to this different vision of life in schools will stimulate the continuation of alliances on behalf of education.

## Professional Practice Schools and Learner-Centered Instructional Practice

A changing view of the learner, a multiplicity of cultures and subcultures clustering in schools, the resulting roles of teachers, and new expectations for pedagogical practice imply entirely new kinds of educating institutions. Schools now teach a skill-based curriculum that is isolated from the ways those skills are used throughout life. Students require a more substantive and functional knowledge base that both prepares them to face practical demands and enables them to advance their own learning and society's as they mature.

A standardized organization of schools assumes that the outcome of every child's education will be a fixed body of knowledge, common to all. This model unrealistically disregards the enormously personal element in learning and the diversity of our society—both impractical and counter-productive outcomes of existing school structures. We have seen how individual the learning process is and how teaching that responds to that individuality unleashes new capabilities among learners by encouraging their involvement in school as active learners.

Professional practice schools offer a systematic alternative to traditional school structures. They are guided by a triple mission to (1) support student learning, (2) improve teaching practice, and (3) educate future teachers (Levine, 1988). These schools respond to the fundamental challenges posed by active learners and an increasingly diverse student population in four ways.

First, professional practice schools address the goal of expanding and integrating students' knowledge by reorienting teaching to center on a core of essential learning processes rather than on narrow lists of skills. Students learn by investigating and applying procedures to solve practical problems in a content-based curriculum. The presence of beginning teachers ensures the influx of fresh ideas and renewed energy to support children with special needs. Moreover, as student teaching centers, professional practice schools have on the faculty enough additional adults, each supervised and monitored, to reduce student–teacher ratios and enable flexible, individual educational options for all students.

Recognizing their responsibility as centers of continuity between home and school, professional practice schools are dedicated to connecting children as well as their communities to new learning opportunities. A fundamental goal is to unify the communities with the larger society through what and how students learn, regardless of ethnic, racial, or social heritage.

The second mission of professional practice schools, to nurture practitioners and reflective teaching, strengthens teachers' responsiveness to children by encouraging continuing critical examination of the goals and processes of teaching. Reflective practitioners, Schön (1988) argues, are collaborative researchers and coaches who seek to understand problems and who create and test new solutions. Teachers' research is a systematic and intentional inquiry conducted by teachers into the effects of their work with children. It is designed to sharpen instructional practice while it imbues teachers with confidence about the quality of their practice. The research takes many forms—journals, essays, oral accounts, exchanges of information, and classroom studies—and it instills a sense of professional efficacy and commitment derived from discovery and the sanctioned search for improvement (Lytle & Cochran-Smith, 1989).

Third, professional practice schools benefit children, today and in the future, through their commitment to the next generation of teachers. Experts and novices together examine, reflect on, and critique each other's work. The process involves closely observing the learner—diagnosis; planned intervention—strategic teaching; and evaluating the outcomes— what students have learned (Leinhardt, 1989).

At present, too many schools try to deliver products—standardized students whose years in school comprise test scores, course loads, and attendance statistics. By contrast, in professional practice schools, children's needs nourish the institution. Such schools are oriented toward students, and they support professionals. In the process, they serve the next generation of teachers and students. Because research and analysis are at the heart of educational practice, professional practice schools are especially responsive to the challenges of teaching students who are at risk, those with varying abilities and disabilities, and those for whom English is not a first language.

Finally, collegiality and collaboration in the broadest sense connect parents as partners with children and teachers in promoting learning. Achieving this connection and trust may be one of the greatest challenges of innovative schools, because parents want and deserve the confidence that their children's education is grounded firmly in a pedagogy of certainty. Neither parents nor teachers countenance the idea of experimenting with children's educational futures. Thus, professional practice schools are not experimental. Their validity derives from the developing research base on which the pedagogy is established. These schools' willingness to inquire and make adjustments is based on the assurance that only effective instruction will survive the scrutiny of many experts.

Professional practice schools include parents in schools in new and more meaningful ways. As partners in educating children, parents respond when teachers solicit their insights and understanding. Their presence in the school and familiarity with its organization promote a level of communication about children, learning, and teaching that, with the research component of the practice schools, enhances the likelihood that the educational program will align correctly with children's evolving needs.

Taken together, the four elements of professional practice schools—

the use of in-depth and interactive teaching strategies, the teacher as re-searcher and analytical practitioner, the expert as a model for the novice, and strong partnerships with parents—demonstrate pedagogy at its best. Along with children and future teachers, seasoned professionals continue to learn and grow. Because they routinely analyze the effects of their prac-tice and model reflection and learning, these teacher leaders offer children their best.

## CONCLUSION

Schools can be places where people of many cultures, communities, and styles joyously work and learn—nondiscriminately, respectfully, and car-ingly. The evidence is clear that schools can be structured so that every child emerges into adulthood having discovered many "possible castles" and "possible worlds" (Bruner, 1986). Similarly, schools can become safe, comfortable places where children realize what it means to belong and to contribute to the community of humankind.

What we know about learning and development implies that pro-ductive schools are inquiry-driven, responsive to student diversity and in-dividuality, and structured to nurture children's powerful motivation and capacity for knowing and learning. These are the most appropriate aims for schools because they are consistent with the nature of learners and with the learning process.

Society can no longer be satisfied with inadequate schools that de-velop the capabilities of only a small proportion of children and leave a quarter or more of the population with an incomplete education. Today's students need to develop abilities that go well beyond what is taught in the traditional curriculum. These skills include speaking, reading, and writing fluently, as well as the capacity to use their knowledge to learn on the job. Students need to apply quantitative know-how to new questions and to production tools that will help answer those questions. Signifi-cantly, they must also learn to work collaboratively in teams, quickly and efficiently building and evaluating alternative solutions to old and new problems.

In short, today's children must find ways to become expert meaning makers in varied and unpredictable contexts. Because they spontaneously learn to derive meaning from the massive array of information they rou-tinely encounter, children learn best in schools that are also diverse and intellectually active—settings that are learner- and learning-centered as well as reflective.

This view of the learner assumes that pedagogical style, instructional activities, and open learning settings are as critical to engaging children in complex thought as is the formal content that is taught. This conception also asserts that all children—especially those of diverse cultural and language heritages—learn best where community building, questioning, exploration, and problem solving are the media of intellectual exchange.

Finally, the underlying assumption of this approach is that children continue to learn when their teachers do too. Teachers are at their best when sustaining their own professional growth in a community that demonstrates its commitment to learning by deeply valuing growth and change. The other authors in this volume explain how such environments create a spirit of perpetual learning that also nurtures the professional development and clinical education of both seasoned and new teachers. There is no better way to ensure expanding learning opportunities for children than through such uninterrupted and systematic improvement of teaching practice.

### NOTES

I am grateful to Pierce Hammond and Judith Meece for their especially helpful suggestions in earlier drafts of this paper, and to sharp-eyed editors Betty Howie and Janet Brown McCracken for their efficient and precise work within short time frames.

1. The Spring 1989 edition of *American Educator* includes several examples of especially sensitive responses to cultural diversity in the curriculum, particularly articles by Atwell, Jackson, and Oxley. Others are offered by Cazden (1988); Gardner, Mason, and Matyas (1989); *Harvard Educational Review* Advisory Board (1988); Heath (1989); and Tharp (1989). For outstanding examples of how community and culture were integrated in progressive schools of the early twentieth century and in open schools in the mid-1960s, see especially Dewey and Dewey (1962), Holt (1964), James (1972), Mayhew and Edwards (1966), Mitchell (1950, 1971), Pratt (1924), Richardson (1964), and Winsor (1973).

2. This vision of teaching and learning extends many of the core ideas of the open education movement of the 1960s (see Ashton-Warner, 1963; Dewey, 1963; Elementary Science Study, 1970; Featherstone, 1971; Hawkins, 1975; Holt, 1964, 1967) that since have become better understood and, to some degree, validated (see Bruner, 1986; Cazden, 1988; Glaser, 1984; Resnick, 1987b; Resnick & Klopfer, 1989). Outstanding essays by distinguished educators whose work spanned this period are found in Biber (1984), Duckworth (1987), and Perrone (1989). Delpit (1986, 1988) and Hale (1982) pose hard questions for well-intentioned educators who may not take into account society's diverse prefer-

ences and needs. (For additional information, see "Sources on Inquiry-Centered Schools" at the end of the references.)

3. Some of the most prominent examples of these programs are the Key and Spectrum schools that are exploring Gardner's (1991) model of multiple intelligences (Blythe & Gardner, 1990). A broad range of high schools are trying Sizer's high school model (Coalition of Essential Schools, 1985; Houston, 1988). Perkins (1986) is working with colleagues at Harvard University and with Gardner to adapt aspects of his knowledge by design. Elementary school models led by Comer (1988a, 1988b), Levin (1988), and Slavin (1989) are receiving particular attention for their focus on content rather than remedial instruction. These examples are rooted in theories that affirm the potential of low-income, minority, and immigrant students who have been least successful in traditional schools.

## REFERENCES

Adelson, J. (1986). *Inventing adolescence: The political psychology of everyday schooling.* New Brunswick, NJ: Transaction Books.

AFT Staff. (1988, Spring). The remarkable impact of creating a school community: One model of how it can be done. An interview with Anne Ratzki. *American Educator, 12*(1), 10–17, 38–43.

Alexander, P. A., & Judy, J. E. (1988). The interaction of domain-specific and strategic knowledge in academic performance. *Review of Educational Research, 58*(4), 375–405.

Almy, M. (1975). *The early childhood educator at work.* New York: McGraw-Hill.

Almy, M., Chittenden, E., & Miller, P. (1966). *Young children's thinking: Studies of some aspects of Piaget's theory.* New York: Teachers College Press.

American Association for the Advancement of Science. (1989). *Science for all Americans: A Project 2061 report on literacy goals in science, mathematics, and technology.* Washington, DC: Author.

Ames, C., & Archer, J. (1988). Achievement goals in the classroom: Students' learning strategies and motivation processes. *Journal of Educational Psychology, 80*(3), 260–267.

Ashton-Warner, S. (1963). *Teacher.* New York: Simon & Schuster.

Association for Supervision and Curriculum Development. (1990a). Focus on assessment. *Update, 32*(7), 1, 3–7.

Association for Supervision and Curriculum Development. (1990b). New curriculum agenda emerges for '90s. *Update, 32*(7), 1–8.

Atwell, N. (1989). Writing workshop. *American Educator, 13*(1), 14–20, 45–50.

Belmont, J. M. (1989). Cognitive strategies and strategic learning: The socio-instructional approach. *American Psychologist, 44*(2), 142–148.

Berlin, G., & Sum, A. (1988). *Toward a more perfect union: Basic skills, poor families and our economic future.* New York: Ford Foundation.

Biber, B. (1984). *Early education and psychological development.* New York: Yale University Press.

Blythe, T., & Gardner, H. (1990). A school for all intelligences. *Educational Leadership, 47*(7), 33–37.

Brandwein, P. F. (1981). *Memorandum: On renewing schooling and education.* New York: Harcourt Brace Jovanovich.

Bransford, J. D., Vye, N. J., Adams, L. T., & Perfetto, G. A. (1989). Learning skills and the acquisition of knowledge. In A. Lesgold & R. Glaser (Eds.), *Foundations for a psychology of education* (pp. 199–250). Hillsdale, NJ: Erlbaum.

Bredekamp, S. (Ed.). (1987). *Developmentally appropriate practice in early childhood programs serving children from birth through age 8.* Washington, DC: National Association for the Education of Young Children.

Brown, A. (1989). Motivation to learn and understand: On taking charge of one's own learning. *Cognition and Instruction, 9*(4), 311–321.

Brown, A. L., Bransford, J. D., Ferrara, R. A., & Campione, J. C. (1983). Learning, remembering, and understanding. In J. H. Flavell & E. M. Markman (Eds.), *Handbook of child psychology: Vol. 3. Cognitive development* (pp. 77–166). New York: John Wiley.

Brown, J. S., Collins, A., & Duguid, P. (1989). Situated cognition and the culture of learning. *Educational Researcher, 18*(1), 32–42.

Bruner, J. (1966). *Toward a theory of instruction.* Cambridge, MA: Harvard University Press.

Bruner, J. (1986). *Actual minds, possible worlds.* Cambridge, MA: Harvard University Press.

Cazden, C. B. (1988). *Classroom discourse: The language of teaching and learning.* Portsmouth, NH: Heinemann.

Ceci, S. J., & Liker, J. (1986). Academic and nonacademic intelligence: An experimental separation. In R. J. Sternberg & R. K Wagner (Eds.), *Practical intelligence: Nature and origins of competence in the everyday world* (pp. 119–143). New York: Cambridge University Press.

Coalition of Essential Schools. (1985). *Prospectus.* Unpublished manuscript, Brown University, Providence, RI.

Cohen, D. H. (1972). *The learning child.* New York: Random House.

Cohen, D. K. (1988). *Teaching practice: Plus ça change . . .* (Issue Paper 88–3). East Lansing, MI: National Center for Research on Teacher Education.

Cole, M., & Cole, S. R. (1989). *The development of children.* New York: Scientific American Books.

Cole, M., Griffin, P., & the Laboratory of Comparative Human Cognition (Eds.). (1987). *Contextual factors in education: Improving science and mathematics education for minorities and women.* Madison: Wisconsin Center for Education Research, School of Education, University of Wisconsin.

Coleman, J. S. (1987). Families and schools. *Educational Researcher, 16*(6), 32–38.

Collins, W. A. (Eds.). (1984). *Development during middle childhood: The years from six to twelve.* Washington, DC: National Academy Press.

Comer, J. P. (1988a). Educating poor minority children. *Scientific American, 259*(5), 42–48.

Comer, J. P. (1988b, November 30). Teaching social skills to at-risk children. *Education Week, 7*(13), 28.

Cremin, L. (1966). *The genius of American education.* New York: Random House.

Cummins, J. (1986). Empowering minority students: A framework for intervention. *Harvard Educational Review, 56*(1), 18–36.

deLone, R. H. (1979). *Small futures: Children, inequality, and the limits of liberal reform.* New York: Harcourt Brace Jovanovich.

Delpit, L. D. (1986). Skills and other dilemmas of a progressive black educator. *Harvard Educational Review, 56*(4), 379–385.

Delpit, L. D. (1988). The silenced dialogue: Power and pedagogy in educating other people's children. *Harvard Educational Review, 58*(3), 280–298.

Dewey, J. (1963). *Experience and education.* Chicago: University of Chicago Press.

Dewey, J., & Dewey, E. (1962). *Schools of tomorrow.* New York: Dutton.

Duckworth, E. (1987). *"The having of wonderful ideas" and other essays on teaching and learning.* New York: Teachers College Press.

Eccles, J. S., & Midgley, C. (1988, November). *Understanding motivation: A developmental approach to person-fit environment.* Paper presented at the National Middle Schools Association Annual Meeting, Denver, CO.

Educational Technology Center, Harvard University. (1985). *Computers, equity and urban schools.* Boston: Author.

Elementary Science Study. (1970). *The ESS reader.* Newton, MA: Education Development Center.

Elkind, D. (1974). *A sympathetic understanding of the child: Birth to sixteen.* Boston: Allyn & Bacon.

Erikson, E. (1950). *Childhood and society* (2nd ed.). New York: Norton.

Eylon, B., & Lynn, M. C. (1988). Learning and instruction: An examination of four research perspectives in science education. *Review of Educational Research, 58*(3), 251–302.

Featherstone, J. (1971). *Schools where children learn.* New York: Liveright.

Fischer, K. W., & Bullock, D. (1984). Cognitive development in school-age children: Conclusions and new directions. In W. A. Collins (Ed.), *Development during middle childhood: The years from six to twelve* (pp. 70–146). Washington, DC: National Academy Press.

Flavell, J. H., & Markman, E. M. (Eds.). (1983). *Cognitive development,* Vol. 3 of *Handbook of child psychology* (P. H. Mussen, Ed.). New York: John Wiley.

Frey, P. S., & Lupart, J. D. (1987). *Cognitive processes in children's learning.* Springfield, IL: Charles C. Thomas.

Gardner, A. L., Mason, C. L., & Matyas, M. L. (1989). Equity, excellence and "just plain good teaching." *American Biology Teacher, 51*(2), 72–77.

Gardner, H. (1985). *Frames of mind: The theory of multiple intelligences.* New York: Basic Books.

Gardner, H. (1991). The school of the future. In J. Brockman (Ed.), *Ways of knowing: Reality Club III* (pp. 199–217). Englewood Cliffs, NJ: Prentice-Hall.

Getzels, J. W. (1977). Paradigm and practice: On the impact of basic research in education. In P. Suppes (Ed.), *Impact of research on education: Some case studies* (pp. 477–522). Washington, DC: National Academy of Education.

Glaser, R. (1984). Education and thinking: The role of knowledge. *American Psychologist, 3*(1), 93–104.

Goodnow, J. J. (1986). Some lifelong everyday forms of intelligent behavior: Organizing and reorganizing. In R. J. Sternberg & R. K. Wagner (Eds.), *Practical intelligence: Nature and origins of competence in the everyday world* (pp. 143–162). New York: Cambridge University Press.

Hale, J. (1982). *Black children: Their roots, culture, and learning styles.* Provo, UT: Brigham Young University Press.

Hamburg, D. A. (1987). *Fundamental building blocks of early life.* New York: Carnegie Corporation.

*Harvard Educational Review* Advisory Board. (1988). Race, racism, and American education: Perspectives of Asian Americans, Blacks, Latinos, and Native Americans [Special Issue]. *Harvard Educational Review, 58*(3).

Hawkins, D. (1970). Messing around with science. In Elementary Science Study, *The ESS reader* (pp. 37–44). Newton, MA: Education Development Center.

Hawkins, F. (1975). *Logic of action: From a teacher's notebook.* New York: Pantheon.

Heath, S. B. (1989). Oral and literate traditions among black Americans living in poverty. *American Psychologist, 44*(2), 367–373.

Hodgkinson, H. (1988). The right schools for the right kids. *Educational Leadership, 45*(5), 11–14.

Holt, J. (1964). *How children fail.* New York: Pitman.

Holt, J. (1967). *How children learn.* New York: Pitman.

Houston, H. M. (1988). Restructuring secondary schools. In A. Lieberman (Ed.), *Building a professional culture in schools* (pp. 109–128). New York: Teachers College Press.

Jackson, A. (1989). Minorities in mathematics: A focus on excellence, not remediation. *American Educator, 12*(1), 22–25.

James, C. (1972). *Young lives at stake: The education of adolescents.* New York: Schocken Books.

Kagan, S. L. (1989, February). Early care and education: Tackling the tough issues. *Phi Delta Kappan, 70*(6), 432–439.

Katz, L. (1977). *Talks with teachers.* Washington, DC: National Association for the Education of Young Children.

Kyle, W. C., Jr. (1984). What became of the curriculum development projects in the 1960's? How effective were they? What did we learn from them that will help teachers in today's classrooms? In D. Holdzkom & P. B. Lutz (Eds.), *Research within reach. Science education: A research-guided response to the concerns of educators* (pp. 3–24). Charleston, WV: Research and Development Interpretation Service, Appalachia Educational Laboratory.

Laboratory of Comparative Human Cognition. (1983). Culture and cognitive development. In P. H. Mussen (Ed.), *Handbook of child psychology: Vol. 1. History, theory, and methods* (pp. 295–356). New York: John Wiley.

Lampert, M. (1985). How do teachers manage to teach? *Harvard Educational Review, 55*(2), 178–194.

Lampert, M. (1989). Choosing and using mathematical tools. In J. Brophy (Ed.), *Teaching for meaningful understanding and self-regulated learning: Vol. 1. Advances in research in teaching.* New York: JAI Press.

Lave, J. (1988). *Cognition in practice: Mind, mathematics and culture in everyday life.* New York: Cambridge University Press.

Leinhardt, G. (1989). Math lessons: A contrast of novice and expert competence. *Journal for Research in Mathematics Education, 20*(1), 52–76.

Lepper, M. R. (1989). Motivational considerations in the study of instruction. *Cognition and Instruction, 9*(4), 289–309.

Lepper, M. R., & Gurtner, J. L. (1989). Children and computers: Approaching the twenty-first century. *American Psychologist, 44*(2), 170–178.

Levin, H. M. (1988). *Accelerated schools for at-risk students* (CPRE Research Report Series RR–010). New Brunswick, NJ: Center for Policy Research in Education, Eagleton Institute of Politics, Rutgers University.

Levin, H. M. (1989). Financing the education of at-risk students. *Educational Evaluation and Policy Analysis, 11*(1), 47–60.

Levine, M. (1988). Introduction. In M. Levine (Ed.), *Professional practice schools: Building a model* (Monograph No. 1). Washington, DC: AFT.

Liben, L. S. (Ed.). (1987). *Development and learning: Conflict or congruence?* Hillsdale, NJ: Erlbaum.

Linney, J. A., & Seidman, E. (1989). The future of schooling. *American Psychologist, 44*(2), 336–340.

Lipsitz, J. S. (1984). *Successful schools for young adolescents.* New Brunswick, NJ: Transaction Press.

Lytle, S. L., & Cochran-Smith, M. (1989). Teacher research: Toward clarifying the concept. *The Quarterly, 11*(2), 1, 22.

Mayhew, K., & Edwards, A. C. (1966). *The Dewey School: The laboratory school at the University of Chicago.* New York: Atherton.

Meece, J., Blumenfeld, P. C., & Puro, P. (1989). *A motivational analysis of elementary school learning environments.* Paper presented at the annual meeting of the American Association for the Advancement of Science, Washington, DC.

Minuchin, P., Biber, B., Shapiro, E., & Zimiles, H. (1969). *The psychological impact of school experience.* New York: Basic Books.

Mitchell, L. S. (1950). *Our children and our schools.* New York: Simon & Schuster.

Mitchell, L. S. (1971). *Young geographers: How they explore the world and how they map the world.* New York: Bank Street College of Education.

National Council of Teachers of Mathematics. (1989). *Curriculum and evaluation standards for school mathematics.* Reston, VA: Author.

Neisser, U. (1976). General, academic, and artificial intelligence. In L. Resnick (Ed.), *The nature of intelligence* (pp. 135–144). Hillsdale, NJ: Erlbaum.

Offer, D., Ostrov, E., & Howard, K. (1981). *The adolescent: A psychological self-portrait.* New York: Basic Books.

Ogbu, J. U. (1987). Opportunity structure, cultural boundaries, and literacy. In J. A. Langer (Ed.), *Language, literacy, and culture: Issues of society and schooling* (pp. 149–177). Norwood, NJ: Ablex.

Oxley, D. (1989). Small is better. *American Educator, 13*(1), 28–37, 51.

Paley, V. (1986). On listening to what the children say. *Harvard Educational Review, 56*(2), 122–131.

Palinscar, A. S., & Brown, A. L. (1984). Reciprocal teaching of comprehension fostering and comprehension monitoring activities. *Cognition and Instruction, I*(2), 117–175.

Perkins, D. (1986). *Knowledge by design.* Hillsdale, NJ: Erlbaum.

Perkins, D., & Simmons, R. (1988). Patterns of misunderstanding: An integrative model for science, math, and programming. *Review of Educational Research, 58*(3), 303–326.

Perrone, V. (1989). *Working papers: Reflections on teachers, schools, and communities.* New York: Teachers College Press.

Piaget, J. (1964). Development and learning. In R. Ripple & V. Rockcastle (Eds.), *Piaget rediscovered* (pp. 7–19). Ithaca, NY: Cornell University Press.

Piaget, J. (1967). *Six psychological studies.* New York: Random House.

Piaget, J. (1972a). *The child and reality: Problems of genetic psychology.* New York: Grossman.

Piaget, J. (1972b). *The principles of genetic epistemology.* New York: Basic Books.

Piaget, J. (1973). *To understand is to invent: The future of education.* New York: Grossman.

Pratt, C. (1924). *Experimental practice in the City and County School.* New York: Dutton.

Presseisen, B. Z. (1987). *Thinking skills throughout the curriculum: A conceptual design.* Bloomington, IN: Pi Lambda Theta, Inc.

Resnick, D. P., & Resnick, L. B. (1977). The nature of literacy. *Harvard Educational Review, 47*(3), 270–385.

Resnick, L. B. (1987a). Constructing knowledge in school. In L. S. Liben (Ed.), *Development and learning: Conflict or congruence?* (pp. 19–50). Hillsdale, NJ: Erlbaum.

Resnick, L. B. (1987b). *Education and learning to think.* Washington, DC: National Academy Press.

Resnick, L. B., & Ford, W. W. (1981). *The psychology of mathematics for instruction.* Hillsdale, NJ: Erlbaum.

Resnick, L. B., & Klopfer, L. E. (Eds.). (1989). *Toward the thinking curriculum: Current cognitive research. 1989 Yearbook of the Association for Supervision and Curriculum Development.* Alexandria, VA: Association for Supervision and Curriculum Development.

Richardson, E. S. (1964). *In the early world.* New York: Pantheon.

Rogoff, B., & Lave, H. (Eds.). (1984). *Everyday cognition: Its development in social context.* Cambridge, MA: Harvard University Press.

Schön, D. A. (1988). Coaching reflective teaching. In P. P. Grimmett & G. L. Erickson (Eds.), *Reflection in teacher education* (pp. 19–30). New York: Teachers College Press.

Schorr, L. B., & Schorr, D. (1988). *Within our reach: Breaking the cycle of disadvantage.* New York: Anchor.

Scribner, S. (1986). Thinking in action: Some characteristics of practical thought. In R. J. Sternberg & R. K. Wagner (Eds.), *Practical intelligence: Nature and origins of competence in the everyday world* (pp. 51–83). New York: Cambridge University Press.

Shanker, A. (1987). The case for public school sponsorship of early childhood education revisited. In S. L. Kagan & E. F. Zigler (Eds.), *Early schooling: The national debate* (pp. 45–64). New Haven, CT: Yale University Press.

Siegler, R. S. (1986). *Children's thinking.* Englewood Cliffs, NJ: Prentice-Hall.

Simmons, R. G., & Blyth, D. A. (1987). *Moving into adolescence: The impact of pubertal change and school context.* New York: Aldine de Gruyter.

Slavin, R. E. (Ed.). (1989). *School and classroom organization.* Hillsdale, NJ: Erlbaum.

Slavin, R. E., & Madden, N. A. (1989). What works for students at risk: A research synthesis. *Educational Leadership, 46*(5), 4–13.

Steinberg, L. (1989). *Adolescence* (2nd ed.). New York: Knopf.

Sternberg, R. J. (1982). Reasoning, problem solving, and intelligence. In R. J. Sternberg (Ed.), *Handbook of human intelligence* (pp. 225–307). New York: Cambridge University Press.

Sternberg, R. J., & Wagner, R. K. (Eds.). (1986). *Practical intelligence: Nature and origins of competence in the everyday world.* New York: Cambridge University Press.

Stodolsky, S. S. (1988). *The subject matters: Classroom activity in math and social studies.* Chicago: University of Chicago Press.

Tanner, J. M. (1978). *Fetus into man: Physical growth from conception to maturity.* Cambridge, MA: Harvard University Press.

Tanner, J. M. (1987). Issues and advances in adolescent growth and development. *Journal of Adolescent Health Care, 8*(6), 470–478.

Tharp, R. G. (1989). Psychocultural variables and constants: Effects on teaching and learning in schools. *American Psychologist, 44*(2), 349–359.

Vygotsky, L. S. (1962). *Thought and language.* Cambridge, MA: MIT Press.

Wagner, R. K., & Sternberg, R. J. (1986). Tacit knowledge and intelligence in the everyday world. In R. J. Sternberg & R. K. Wagner (Eds.), *Practical intelligence: Nature and origins of competence in the everyday world* (pp. 51–83). New York: Cambridge University Press.

Walters, J. M., & Gardner, H. (1986). The theory of multiple intelligences: Some issues and answers. In R. J. Sternberg & R. K. Wagner (Eds.), *Practical intelligence: Nature and origins of competence in the everyday world* (pp. 163–182). New York: Cambridge University Press.

Weinberg, R. A. (1989). Intelligence and IQ: Landmark issues and great debates. *American Psychologist, 44*(2), 98–104.

Wertsch, J. V. (1985). *Vygotsky and the social formation of mind.* New York: Cambridge University Press.

White, S. H., & Siegel, A. W. (1984). Cognitive development in time and space.

In B. Rogoff & J. Lave (Eds.), *Everyday cognition: Its development in social context* (pp. 238–277). Cambridge, MA: Harvard University Press.

Winsor, C. (1973). *Experimental schools revisited.* New York: Agathon.

Zigler, E. F. (1987, September). *A solution to the nation's child care crisis: The school for the twenty-first century.* Paper delivered at the tenth anniversary of the Bush Center in Child Development and Social Policy, New Haven, CT.

Zigler, E. F., Kagan, S. L., & Klugman, E. (1983). *Children, families, and government.* New York: Cambridge University Press.

## SOURCES ON INQUIRY-CENTERED SCHOOLS

Blackie, J. (1971). *Inside the primary school.* New York: Schocken.

Carmichael, L. (1981). *McDonogh 15: Becoming a school.* New York: Avon.

Combs, A. W., Blume, R. A., Newman, A. I., & Wass, H. L. (1974). *The professional education of teachers: A humanistic approach to teacher preparation.* Boston: Allyn & Bacon.

Dennison, G. (1969). *The lives of children: The story of the First Street School.* New York: Vintage.

Devaney, K. (1974). *Developing open education in America: A review of theory and practice in the public schools.* Washington, DC: National Association for the Education of Young Children.

Isaacs, S. (1971). *The children we teach.* New York: Schocken.

Kohl, H. (1967). *36 children.* New York: New American Library.

Montessori, M. (1967). *The discovery of the child.* Notre Dame, IN: Fides Publishers.

Pestalozzi, J. H. (1827). *Letters on early education.* London: Sherwood, Gilbert, & Piper.

Pratt, C. (1948). *I learn from children.* New York: Simon & Schuster.

Rice, J. (1892–1893). Our public school system [series of articles]. *Forum, 14;* and *Forum, 15.*

Tolstoy, L. (1967). *Tolstoy on education* (L. Weiner, Trans.). Chicago: University of Chicago Press.

Weber, L. (1971). *The English infant school and informal education.* Englewood Cliffs, NJ: Prentice-Hall.

Whitehead, A. N. (1929). *The aims of education.* New York: Macmillan.

# 3 | Establishing Professional Schools for Teachers

## MARY M. KENNEDY

Drawing on the teaching hospital analogy, many education reformers dream of a place where teachers can study and learn about teaching *as they are teaching*. The envisioned "professional development school" (or, as used elsewhere in this book, "professional practice school") would be a functioning elementary or secondary school with a teacher education program more rigorous than the current student teaching programs are, yet more practice-oriented than the current university programs for teaching often are.

Though the concept of a professional development school is intriguing, the details of its operation have not yet been worked out. A great deal more dialogue and debate are needed to transform the dream into a workable blueprint. Much of that dialogue will address two important points: the nature of professional expertise that is to be developed in these schools, and the processes by which professional expertise is developed. This chapter contributes to the dialogue by examining both of these issues—the nature of professional expertise and the process by which it is developed—and presents an argument for a particular professional development strategy.

The chapter is divided into four principal sections, the first of which examines the nature of professional expertise. The second section focuses on the ways in which the development of such expertise can be fostered, particularly with respect to the most prevalent in-school method of preparing teachers—student teaching. The third section draws upon the first two to derive a set of goals for professional development programs, and the fourth section applies the criteria implicit in these goals to a few examples of learning opportunities that could be offered to novice teachers.

## THE NATURE OF PROFESSIONAL EXPERTISE

Professional development schools would have an easy time of it if their goal were to provide professional *knowledge*. It is easy to tell someone

63

that water boils at 212 degrees, and not too difficult to get them to re-member that. With these tasks accomplished, we can say that our learner has acquired some knowledge. We can also provide more elaborate knowledge by pointing out that boiling water kills resident bacteria, and we can ensure that our learner remembers this as well. The difficulty comes when we want to ensure that our learner will actually boil water when it is necessary to do so. To perform this act, our learner must (1) translate the knowledge from a sentence form into an action form, (2) adopt a goal of eliminating bacteria, and (3) recognize situations where this action will contribute to this goal. When these things happen, we say our learner has developed expertise. When knowledge is connected to situations—when it ceases to be a repository and becomes dynamic and operational—it has been transformed into expertise.

In an earlier review of professional education literature, I identified four forms of expertise and found that knowledge contributes to each in a unique way (Kennedy, 1987). One form of expertise consists of the ap-plication of technical skills. Doctors use technical skills when they sew up wounds, architects when they draw blueprints, and teachers when they suppress student disruptions. Another form of expertise consists of ap-plying concepts, theories, and principles. Principles are usually in the form "if *x*, then *y*," or "to accomplish *x*, do *y*." The task of the practi-tioner is to identify the appropriate principle for each particular situation and then apply it.

The third form of expertise consists of the ability to critically analyze a situation and to generate multiple interpretations of it. Lawyers do this when they identify the potential legal precedents that could apply to a case, teachers when they generate hypotheses for why a child is reluctant to participate, and movie critics when they consider various analogies that could be used to characterize a particular film. Rather than finding *the* appropriate principle to apply to each case, critical analysts are aware of multiple and sometimes competing principles and concepts that could be applied to the same situations. Their task is to examine *both* the prin-ciples *and* the situation, and to select the most appropriate match. Criti-cal analysis is a form of expertise especially relevant to professions whose "actions" are primarily intellectual rather than physical—historians, lit-erary critics, or lawyers, for instance.

Finally, expertise can consist of deliberate action. Like critical anal-ysis, deliberate action entails multiple interpretations of a situation. But it goes beyond analysis and yields an action. As a form of expertise, delib-erate action recognizes that there may be multiple goals in any given sit-uation, and that multiple, conflicting principles may apply to the same case. While the critical analyst chooses among alternative ways of interpreting a case, the deliberate actor chooses among alternative *goals* that may be sought in a given situation. These goals provide alternative frames of reference from which actions can be chosen.

Deliberate actions entail guesses as to what the likely outcomes of actions will be, and choices about actions and outcomes that are based on those guesses. It is the actor's experiences with this or similar cases that enable him or her to make these guesses about outcomes, and it is these guesses that make it possible to choose a goal from among many that could be focused on. For instance, the lawyer who recognizes several potential precedents in a case uses her experience with this particular judge to choose the precedent—and, concurrently, a goal for the case—that is most likely to succeed with this judge. The teacher with the reluctant child chooses his action on the basis of his prior experience with this child, and the architect revises her design on the basis of prior encounters with similar landscapes.

These four forms of expertise are distinguishable by the way in which knowledge is linked to action. When expertise consists of technical skills, the knowledge *is* the action. When expertise consists of applying concepts, theories, or principles, knowledge exists independent of action and provides the decision rules for choosing an action. In either of these two cases, the knowledge is codified and identifiable, and can be imparted to the practitioner. This is not true of the latter two forms of expertise. In these, actions are not guided by stable decision rules. Instead, the frames of reference one might rely on may contradict one another. To select one, the practitioner critically examines *both* the knowledge *and* the situation in order to produce a good match. In the case of deliberate action, the frame of reference may be a goal rather than a theory, but the choice of goal entails critical examination of a range of potential actions and their consequences and a range of potential goals. And just as a critical analyst may change frames of reference if he or she cannot adequately interpret the situation, a deliberate actor may change the original goal if it cannot be accomplished.

The first two forms of expertise imply that there is an explicit body of content that should be imparted to the novice. I will use the term *content* to refer to the technical skills, concepts, theories, or principles that are contained in codified bodies of professional knowledge. These two forms of expertise depend on content that can be defined in advance, organized into a curriculum, given to novices, and later applied by them. For these forms of expertise, professional preparation would consist of giving novices the content and then showing them when and how to apply it.

The role of content in the latter two forms of expertise is less clear.

Content is not automatically applied to situations; instead, critical analysts and deliberate actors seek optimal matches between concepts and principles, on one side, and the situations they encounter, on the other. Both analysts and deliberators must have access to content, but they also must know how to examine the content, how to examine the situation, and how to examine the match between the two.

And because the criteria for goodness-of-fit between frames of reference or goals, on one hand, and the situations encountered, on the other, are themselves a matter of judgment, these forms of expertise require more than knowledge. They require an ability to engage in such analyses, a desire to engage in such analyses, and a disposition to continually seek better solutions. These two forms of expertise cannot be developed simply by giving professionals relevant knowledge. Instead, novices must be *transformed* into people who are inclined to critically examine their own practice and to search for ways to improve it.

Of all the forms of expertise, the most difficult in which to identify content is deliberate action. Deliberation is based not only on whatever codified skills, principles, or concepts have been formally transmitted, but also on one's own experiences in this and analogous situations. Each learner deduces morals from each story he or she encounters, and draws on these morals in future deliberations. These experiences not only contribute to interpretations of future experiences but also to interpretations of *previously learned* codified knowledge (Kennedy, 1983). Everything—thoughts about appropriate goals, interpretations of codified knowledge, and estimates of the probable consequences of various actions—evolves over time with new experiences and new thoughts about these experiences. This developmental process makes the content and character of expertise-as-deliberate-action very difficult to define, for deliberators each continually reconstruct their own knowledge bases as they encounter new experiences and re-examine goals. Thus, what counts as "knowledge" varies from individual to individual even within a profession. And what counts as an appropriate goal in any given situation may also vary depending on which member of the profession encounters the situation.

## FOSTERING DIFFERENT KINDS OF EXPERTISE

Professional development can include an infinite number of activities, some better than others, some more suited to certain forms of expertise than others. In what follows, I briefly review research on ways of fostering different forms of expertise.

First, with respect to technical skills, there exists a relatively large body of research (Joyce & Showers, 1980) that indicates that these skills are not acquired casually. Four things must occur.

1. The skills need to be explicitly defined and their purposes explained to the novice
2. The skills need to be demonstrated to the novice
3. The novice needs an opportunity to practice the skills and to receive feedback
4. These first three events must occur in controlled environments designed specifically to teach these skills, rather than in the unpredictable world of real practice

Only after novices have mastered the skills in a sheltered environment, Joyce and Showers argue, should they practice the skills in real classrooms.

While there is less research on teaching novices to apply concepts and principles, a widely accepted conventional wisdom does exist regarding the development of this form of expertise. It is generally assumed that novices first need to learn the concepts, theories, and principles, and only later learn to apply them. That is, it would not be useful for students to practice their profession or to observe practitioners before they have learned the relevant codified knowledge. Most university-based professional schools, whether they prepare businesspeople, doctors, social workers, or engineers, reflect this view: They offer a year or two of courses in the scientific bases of the profession, sometimes accompanied by laboratory courses that enable students to apply the concepts or principles, and at the end of the program they provide an internship during which students presumably learn to apply the content to practice.

We also have a model available for fostering critical analysis. This is the form of expertise that is most heavily emphasized in law schools, where students engage for three years in almost nothing but critical analysis. They read and analyze appellate court decisions and debate them in class. Their professors raise questions and objections, and encourage students to question one another. The goal of law schools is to make students "think like lawyers"—to be critical analysts. Their method of instruction is such that content—legal concepts, principles, and precedents—is embedded in the analytical tasks, so that students absorb it in the process of learning the process. Because the process of critical analysis determines which frames of reference are most relevant and why, the analytical task is difficult to separate from the content. By the time budding lawyers have analyzed cases for three years, they have been transformed into critical analysts. They think like lawyers. And, though they have acquired a body of knowledge, they have not acquired that knowledge independent of the analytical process. They have acquired it through the analytical process.

Much less is known about how to foster deliberate action. Presumably, one would want to give novices an experience similar to that received by lawyers; they should receive extended, intense practice analyzing their own actions and the effects of those actions, with a mentor constantly challenging their reasoning. The training that Schön (1983) describes for architects satisfies this requirement: The novice architect designs and redesigns the same building, trying it many different ways, and applying a variety of criteria to his or her efforts, all with the aid of a critical mentor. Schön (1987) argues that, to be effective, the mentor's questions and challenges must come at the very moment the novice is deliberating, and that moment usually occurs when the actor is in the situation. But the architect's actions occur on the drawing board, not in a classroom with other actors. A teacher's actions are nearly all interactions. It is not possible to re-teach the same math lesson to the same students several times, examining the merits of each successive trial with one's mentor. Actions and situations are necessarily nonrepeatable. Nor can a teacher engage in intense analytical dialogue while in the flow of action. And if the conversation occurs later on, much of the detail of the event may already be lost to memory; consequently, some interpretations may be lost as well. Analysis requires the action to be temporarily frozen.

Many authors have criticized existing teacher preparation programs on the ground that these programs fail to foster expertise in the form of deliberate action. Probably the earliest critic was John Dewey (1904/1965), who distinguished the control of the "intellectual methods" of teaching from the mastery of skills, and introduced the notion of laboratory schools into teacher education. Dewey used the term *laboratory* because he intended these schools to be places of experimentation, where novice teachers would be encouraged to try different actions and to evaluate the consequences of those actions. Several contemporary authors have emphasized the same tension that Dewey was concerned about. Arnstine (1975), for instance, complains about apprenticeship as a means of learning to teach on the grounds that apprenticeship results only in copying the behaviors that are observed, whereas the goal of preparation should be to cultivate relevant understandings and dispositions. Similarly, Eggleston (1985) notes a tension between novices' short-term need for immediate coping skills and their long-term need to incorporate critical reflection into their practice.

There is ample evidence that, during the first few weeks of teaching, usually during student teaching, novices do change their views substantially. But the evidence does not suggest that they become better deliberators. Instead, it suggests that they become less theoretical, less ideal, more practical, and more control-oriented (Haberman, 1982). Research on the nature of student teaching experiences has suggested several hypotheses for why this is so. Tabachnik, Popkowitz, and Zeichner (1979–80), for instance, found that student teachers' activities were limited to mechanical teaching of short-term skills: testing, grading, management, or recitation. Furthermore, student teachers had little control over their activities. If opportunities and responsibilities are curtailed in these ways, novices have little opportunity to deliberate over, or to try, alternative courses of action.

On the other hand, Hodges (1982) found that novice reading teachers regressed when they had entire responsibility for their own teaching—that is, when there was no cooperating teacher in the classroom to curtail the novice's responsibility. In interviews, the novices attributed their behavior to the press for classroom survival, to limited time, and to their inability to recall, when they needed it, the formal content they had learned in their university methods courses. Thus, as a learning opportunity, student teaching may fail if the novice has so little responsibility that there is no opportunity for experimentation and for deliberation about these experiments, and it may fail if the novice has so much responsibility that he or she is overwhelmed to the point where deliberation is not possible.

With regard to the guidance novices receive, McIntyre and Killian (1986) found that cooperating teachers give very little feedback to student teachers, and McNergney and Francis (1986) found that supervisors tended to be nonanalytical in their interactions with student teachers, concentrating instead on being supportive. Tom (1972) found that supervisor interactions with novices were quite predictable—praise something, then offer constructive criticism, then end on a positive note—but that there was no substantive continuity from one supervisory visit to the next. Furthermore, visits were infrequent, and supervisors had no sense for whether the behaviors they observed were representative of the novices' general strategies. Zeichner and Liston (1987) found that even in a program that strongly emphasized reflective teaching, not all supervisors engaged in the kind of interactions that one would expect to foster such expertise. Only 19% of seminar discourse indicated critical reflection, and many supervisors were more oriented toward technical skills or toward personal growth—that is, finding a style that "works for you"—than toward stimulating critical analysis or deliberate action. Finally, Arthur Powell (personal communication, March 1987) found that the curricula of seminars accompanying private school internships usually lacked any thematic focus and instead offered novices an eclectic mix of "stuff." One session might be on the use of computers, another on assertive discipline, another on cultural literacy.

## THE TASK OF PROFESSIONAL DEVELOPMENT SCHOOLS

In the first section of this chapter, I identified four forms of expertise—technical skills, conceptual/theoretical skills, critical analysis, and deliberate action—each of which entails a unique way of transforming knowledge from sentences into action. It should be apparent that these forms of expertise are not independent of one another: Most professions require all of them, and most practitioners possess all of them to varying degrees. Nevertheless, it is useful to separate them when thinking about professional development, for these forms of expertise imply different strategies of professional preparation. In thinking about the unique features of professional development schools relative to universities or other contexts for teacher preparation, I draw two conclusions.

1. The form of expertise *most appropriate* for professional development schools to foster is deliberate action. Deliberate actions are based in experience, and expertise in deliberate action is most likely to be developed by experience in deliberating; that is, experience in establishing real goals in real situations, working toward those goals, and learning from these experiences which goals can and can't be met in which kinds of circumstances. The most salient feature of the professional development school, relative to the university, is that it provides the real experiences needed to begin deliberating about practice.

2. The form of expertise *most necessary* for professional development schools to attend to is also deliberate action. For even if professional development schools did not try to foster deliberate action, novices would still think about their experiences and would still draw conclusions that would influence their future actions—yet their conclusions might be flawed. When failing to meet a goal, they might assume the goal was not appropriate, when in fact their method of approaching it was the problem. Real experiences happen fast, and novices may not be able to grasp all the relevant aspects of their experiences without assistance. Without guidance, novices may draw many erroneous conclusions about their practice, and these conclusions may influence their practice for years to come. Not only are professional development schools particularly suited to fostering deliberate action, therefore; they have an obligation to do so, since novices will begin to develop models of practice, either well or poorly, when they begin to practice.

Yet deliberate action is also the most difficult form of expertise to foster, for two reasons. First, the process of deliberation is normally a private one, and it is often based on experiences that are not witnessed by other teachers. Further, practitioners may ruminate about their experiences at odd hours of the day, when other practitioners are not available to review or influence these conclusions. Second, the nature of practice is such that practitioners may draw conclusions that are hard to articulate, and may base these conclusions on experiences that are hard to describe. It is not clear how a supervisor or mentor can hope to improve a novice's deliberations, without being able to monitor or influence those conclusions.

This in turn suggests some criteria by which learning opportunities for teachers could be assessed. In evaluating the potential of a professional development program, we might look for evidence that they meet the following conditions, which may be necessary to foster deliberate action in teaching.

1. Novices must have *responsibilities that require deliberation:* responsibilities for establishing their own goals and for selecting their own actions. The act of deliberation involves defining the situation and selecting both goals and actions to suit it. Yet Tabachnik, Popkowitz, and Zeichner (1979–80) found that student teachers' tasks were limited to relatively well-defined activities assigned by the cooperating teacher. In these circumstances, student teachers have no opportunity to engage in the central task of deliberation. The task of professional development programs must be to ensure that novices have this responsibility.

2. Novices must have the *opportunity to deliberate.* They need both the time and the knowledge to judge their goals, their actions, and the consequences of their actions in light of recognized concepts, theories, and principles of teaching and learning. This second criterion complements the first. While it is important for novices to take responsibility for situations, the evidence from Hodges's (1982) study suggests that, when given full responsibility for classrooms, novices were overwhelmed by their responsibilities and were unable to recall the codified knowledge they had learned in their methods courses. If novices are to learn to deliberate over their own goals and actions, they must have both the time to deliberate and the content—that is, the theories, concepts, and principles—needed to interpret situations, establish goals, and evaluate the consequences of past and proposed actions.

3. Supervisors or mentors must be able to *monitor novices' deliberations*—to monitor their interpretations of their experiences and their conclusions about their goals, their actions, and the consequences of

those actions. Novices routinely interpret and draw conclusions about their experiences, but we do not know what those conclusions are, for the current system of supervision does not enable supervisors to learn what their student teachers are concluding about their experiences. Consequently, almost any conclusions, erroneous or fruitful, will remain with the novice when he or she leaves student teaching to take a full-time position. Even if these conclusions cannot be readily influenced, professional development schools have an obligation to monitor the views that novices are forming and to prevent teachers with erroneous or indefensible views from continuing in the profession.

4. Supervisors or mentors must be able to *influence novices' deliberations* by offering contrary evidence and rival hypotheses, and by criticizing novices' hypotheses in light of recognized concepts, theories, and principles of teaching and learning. The evidence reviewed above suggests that much of the guidance provided to novices is nonanalytical and tends to provide support rather than critique. If this is true then supervisors are probably not influencing either the conclusions or the deliberative process used to reach those conclusions. Yet if conclusions about past actions and their consequences are contributing to future decisions, supervisors must somehow ensure that novices are aware of alternative interpretations of their early experiences, that they understand how their actions would be judged according to a variety of recognized standards, and that they are aware of outcomes foregone by their choice of goals and actions.

But how supervisors are to influence deliberations is not at all clear, for, by definition, deliberate action renders professional concepts and principles relative to specific situations. When expertise is defined as the application of recognized concepts or principles, it is easy to define standards for professional practice and easy for observers to judge the appropriateness of a novice's actions. But when decisions depend on how one interprets the situation, the observer loses authority for judging the appropriateness of any particular action. If professional development schools are to foster deliberate action, they must do so in a way that promotes professional standards while at the same time acknowledging that situations can be viewed in multiple ways, and that it may be legitimate to alter goals to fit situations. This leads to the fifth criterion.

5. Supervisors or mentors must *infuse content* into novices' deliberations about experiences and actions. Content—that is, professional skills, concepts, theories, and principles—provides the standards for judging others' practice, the framework for establishing one's own goals, and the criteria for evaluating the consequences of one's own past and proposed actions. Content enables self-regulation as well as the grounds

for critical self-assessment. Consequently, professional development schools have an obligation to infuse skills, concepts, principles, and theory into novices' deliberations about their actions and the consequences of their actions. Just as lawyers learn, through the process of critical analysis, how to find and judge content that may be relevant to a case, teachers must learn through their own deliberations to define and judge content that may be relevant to their goals and actions.

This last point may seem contrary to the thrust of deliberate action: I argued earlier that content was important when expertise consisted of the application of skills, concepts, and principles, but that critical analysis and deliberation required an inclination toward analysis and the ability to reject content when it was not appropriate to a situation. But content provides the stuff of deliberation: the frames of reference for interpreting situations, the value judgments for selecting goals, and the principles for choosing among competing actions. Even a decision to reject a particular principle or concept requires awareness of the principle and how it could be applied to a situation. It is competition among various contents that makes deliberation rigorous. Finally, content provides the language for describing and interpreting experiences. If each teacher were left to deliberate in private, conversations among teachers would resemble a Tower of Babel.

## EXAMPLES OF PROFESSIONAL DEVELOPMENT SCHOOL ACTIVITIES

The preceding sections of this chapter have put forward an argument both for the kind of expertise professional development schools should try to foster and for how that kind of expertise is most likely to be fostered. But the principles are still at a rather abstract level. To illustrate how they might be used in designing a professional development program, I now apply these criteria to a few specific learning opportunities that have been or could be used to help teachers learn to teach. I try to evaluate such learning opportunity for its potential in fostering deliberate action, based on the five criteria listed in the previous section.

### Learning How Children Learn by Tutoring One Child

Tutoring involves many aspects of teaching—developing goals, designing lessons, implementing lessons, diagnosing the student's understanding of the material, revising plans, and revising goals. Consequently, tutoring meets our first criterion listed above: It enables novices to develop their own strategies. And since tutoring itself would require only an hour or less each day, the novice would have time to deliberate—our second criterion. To satisfy the third and fourth criteria, we need a mechanism that enables the supervisor to monitor and influence the novice's conclusions. This could occur if the supervisor met regularly with the novice to discuss the novice's "case," criticized the novice's activities in light of the concepts and principles of child development, and occasionally observed the novice tutoring the child in order to provide rival hypotheses and contradictory evidence from those observations. Since the purpose of the tutoring is to help novices learn more about how children learn, and to recognize signs of learning and signs of confusion, the project satisfies our fifth criterion. Part of the supervisor's job is to infuse knowledge of cognitive development into these circumstances.

Because such a project might be construed as a variant of ordinary guided practice, it might be instructive to review the ways in which it differs from ordinary guided practice. First, it establishes the novice's responsibility in a very different way. Student teachers can be hampered by too little responsibility when their cooperating teachers hold the real authority in the classroom, and by too much responsibility when they are left in complete charge of the classroom. Tutoring avoids both of these pitfalls. The tutoring novice has full responsibility for the tutoring project, a feature that is important to deliberate action. But the responsibility is limited to one student, one subject, and one hour or half-hour a day, so that the student teacher has ample time to digest and deliberate over his or her actions. Second, in ordinary guided practice the student teacher's supervisor interacts with the student teacher only occasionally, when he or she observes a teaching episode, whereas the tutoring novice's supervisor is involved in ongoing conversation with the novice about the tutoring project. Consequently, the tutoring novice's supervisor knows the development of the novice's reasoning over time and can respond to that rather than to random events he or she happens to observe. Finally, the student teacher's supervisor has no substantive agenda, so that the supervisor's response to the student's teaching episode is unpredictable and most likely unrelated to the student teacher's intentions and interests in the episode. In contrast, the tutoring novice's supervisor has a clear agenda. It is to enhance the novice's ability to evaluate goals and actions in light of a particular set of concepts and principles.

It should also be clear that the tutor's supervisor is not an ordinary teacher. This is a person who is thoroughly grounded in the content—the theory, concepts, and principles—but who also is well grounded in experience and aware of the contradictions experiences may offer to theory. Finally, this is an individual who is experienced in fostering deliberate action in adult learners.

**Learning Subject Matter Through a Mathematics Study Group**

The second learning activity is a mathematics study group. All group members are engaged in teaching mathematics, though they may be teaching it to very different kinds of students. The group could meet weekly and discuss issues that have arisen about mathematics in their teaching. A member may describe a problem she encountered explaining a particular concept to her students, and her realization that she really did not understand the concept herself. The group may then examine that mathematical concept in depth and discuss alternative ways of thinking about it and of helping students understand it. Another member may raise questions about a section of a math textbook and its applicability to particular mathematical concepts. As members deliberate, the study group leader interjects lessons about mathematics when it is apparent that novices do not understand the content, and inserts mathematical criteria into discussions about evaluating textbooks, explaining concepts, or sequencing lessons.

The study group in mathematics could be construed to be a variant of ordinary internship seminars, but it is not an open-ended conversation. Instead, it focuses on a particular content area and encourages deliberation within that area. It also satisfies our five criteria. Because members of the study group are practicing, they have an opportunity to establish their own goals and strategies and to evaluate their actions and the consequences of those actions. Second, the weekly conversations enable the group leader to monitor and challenge their conclusions. The content focus of the study group enables the leader to critique the members' goals and actions in light of these concepts and principles.

**Learning About School–Community Relations Through a Case Study**

Professional development schools could also rely on case histories of real or hypothetical situations, for they cannot assume that "good" examples will naturally present themselves each year. Imagine, for instance, a problem that would foster deliberation about the relationship between school, parents, and society. The problem is multifaceted. It involves a recently rezoned secondary school whose student body has changed from a uniformly white, lower-income population to a population that is heterogeneous racially and in family income. Many parents are dissatisfied with their children's new school, and several have threatened to remove their children if the district does not return them to their original schools. Among the new students are many who belong to a particularly strict religion, and teachers have noticed that other students have been cruel and aloof toward these students. During this unrest, a group of middle- and upper-income parents has protested the school's social studies curriculum, arguing that it is not relevant to their youngsters' backgrounds. The textbook they want adopted was recently rejected by the school district's curriculum committee on the basis of research evidence regarding its accuracy. The principal of this school is a strong instructional leader who is respected by the teachers, but she is unable to garner confidence from parents. The problem posed to novice teachers, who all teach social studies, is to develop a package of strategies that will resolve these problems. The novices form a committee and meet regularly to develop their plan. A supervisor meets with them, monitors their thinking, and challenges their ideas with contrary evidence and rival hypotheses.

Though the problem is hypothetical, it does require novices to choose among competing goals and competing actions—to deliberate. Further, because a supervisor attends the committee meetings, he is able to monitor the conclusions novices draw and to challenge those conclusions. Finally, the supervisor can insert findings from research on parent–school relations and political science concepts related to governance in education and can stimulate novices to use these concepts and principles to estimate the likely outcome of their plans and to judge the appropriateness of their goals and strategies.

## Learning How One's Own Practices Influence Students Through Video Deliberations

This learning opportunity represents an attempt to improve the ordinary internship seminar so that it is more likely to enhance deliberate action. The procedure works as follows. First, novices are videotaped as they teach once a week. They view these videotapes of themselves and identify one event they are proud of and one event they are dissatisfied with. They establish goals for improving particular aspects of their teaching. One novice may want to decrease her use of leading questions, while another aims to improve the number and variety of examples and analogies he uses. When novices meet weekly for their seminar, they must be prepared to show one another their good and bad practices, to explain their assessment of these actions, and to define and justify their goals. Other novices as well as the seminar leader may question a presenting novice's reasoning, pointing out evidence in the tape that the presenting novice overlooked or suggesting alternative hypotheses to account for the events. The novice's goals provide substantive continuity from week to week, and the tapes enable participants to see things in the events that they otherwise might not be able to see.

These video deliberations also satisfy our five criteria. The novices deliberate about their own actions and their own goals; the seminar leader is able to monitor and challenge their conclusions about these events. Further, she is able to bring into the conversation concepts, theories, and research findings about teaching techniques, thereby encouraging novices to use this content in their assessment of their own experiences and their own goals.

### Learning Group Management by Organizing a Class Activity with No Instruction Involved

My last example requires the novice to organize an activity that does not involve instruction. The activity could be a game at recess, a hike, a trip to the zoo, or a cake sale. The reason I de-emphasize instruction in this example is that this project is intended to foster deliberation about classroom management; consequently the project is designed to minimize attention to other issues.

This example does not satisfy my criteria as well as the other examples have. Because novices design their own projects, it engages them in deliberation. But a supervisor may not be able to monitor or to challenge their conclusions. If the novice's project is a one-time event, rather than an ongoing event, the supervisor may be unable to respond to the novice's conclusions while the novice is still deliberating. The supervisor can discuss the novices' plans with them beforehand and help them examine their ideas, and he can discuss their assessment of the events afterward. But once the event is finished, his critique may have no consequence because there is no future action or goal to be reconsidered in light of his challenges. Consequently this project does not satisfy all the criteria. There may be strategies that can make it work better, such as requiring novices to write a paper describing how they would do this event again if they had the opportunity to repeat it, or establishing a system where the novice actually had repeated opportunities to do comparable activities in different classrooms.

### CONCLUSIONS

Professional development schools must help novices deliberate better—help them formulate more hypotheses to account for the situations they encounter, help them apply more varied standards to their actions, and help them engage in a more critical analysis of the goals they establish for themselves. To do this, professional development schools must see that each novice has an opportunity to engage in deliberate action—to take actions that are deliberate and to deliberate about those actions both before and after they have been taken. They must also find ways to monitor novices' thoughts and respond to them. When they respond, they must find ways to infuse content into novices' deliberations, for it is content— the professional concepts, theories, and principles—that provides the criteria for judging actions and their consequences. The two central tasks of the professional development school—improving novices' deliberate action and imparting usable content—are actually the same task, for deliberations are improved by infusing content into them, and usable content is imparted by infusing it into deliberations.

This chapter offers a frame of reference for planning professional development schools and for evaluating various learning opportunities that could be provided for teachers. The examples presented here are intended to be illustrative of the kinds of opportunities professional development schools might offer to novice teachers. They are by no means inclusive of all possibilities. But careful consideration of these illustrations raises a number of issues about the potential of professional development schools.

One is that the creation of appropriate learning opportunities may introduce serious and complicated staffing problems. Though I sought examples that fostered deliberate action within the context of practice, most of the learning opportunities described here occur outside regular classrooms. Furthermore, the novices are not engaged in full-time teaching activities. That means that professional development schools may find that the goals of fostering expertise conflict with the goal of educating pupils. If novices are given full responsibility for only limited portions of children's education, then experienced teachers must be available to take responsibility for the remainder of the children's education. Furthermore, still others must be available to work with novices in their deliberations. Finally, most of these examples require long-term intense interaction with a supervisor or mentor. Thus, one important implication of the argument presented here is that these programs would be far more costly and far more difficult to develop than conventional teaching internships are. They require at least the following:

*Staffing patterns that provide*
- Limited and focused responsibilities for novices so that they can deliberate at length about the responsibilities they do have
- Full-time teachers in every classroom so that novices are never overwhelmed by full responsibility for a class

- Full-time novice supervisors or mentors who have both content expertise and expertise in helping adults learn
- A rather large complement of supervisors or mentors, each with his or her own area of content expertise
- A ratio of novices to supervisors or mentors that enables supervisors to spend ample time with each novice

*An organization that provides*
- A mechanism for coordinating novice activities with regular classroom routines in a way that does not interrupt the regular teacher's rhythm yet enables novices to do such things as tutor a child, organize a hike, or regularly teach the math lesson
- A mechanism for coordinating novice activities to ensure that each novice receives an adequate portfolio of learning opportunities, and a method for rotating novices through them all

*Program policies that provide*
- A method of monitoring novices, a set of criteria for satisfactory progress, a method of flagging those who do not respond well, and a procedure for handling these cases
- Criteria for selecting supervisors or mentors that recognizes their content knowledge and their ability to teach adults, rather than their years of experience teaching or their formal degree (An important issue to be determined is whether or not these mentors must themselves be practicing teachers, or whether they can be, for instance, university professors.)

Another issue implied in this analysis is that if schools are to take seriously the task of preparing novices to teach, they will need to give as much attention to the education of teachers as they now give to the education of pupils. The conversion of an ordinary school into a professional development school will entail a considerable amount of thought about the curriculum that will be offered to novice teachers and to the kinds of learning opportunities that will be offered. If new staff and new novices are placed in schools without attention to the specific activities that will occur, the result may not lead to the kind of learning that would be most beneficial to novices.

Yet a third implication of this analysis is that such learning opportunities are indeed possible. They will not appear without serious attention to staffing, organization, and policy, and they will not appear without attention to the curriculum and learning opportunities that should be offered to novices, but they can be developed. And if they are developed, they will foster a form of expertise that has long been desired in teachers, but that has been elusive to teacher educators and other educational reformers.

## REFERENCES

Arnstine, D. (1975). Apprenticeship as the miseducation of teachers. *Philosophy of Education 1975: Proceedings of the thirty-first annual meeting of the Philosophy of Education Society* (pp. 113–123). San Jose, CA: Society for Studies in Philosophy and Education.

Dewey, J. (1965). The relation of theory to practice in education. In M. L. Borrowman (Ed.), *Teacher education in America: A documentary history.* New York: Teachers College Press. (Original work published 1904)

Eggleston, J. (1985). Subject centred and school based teacher training in the postgraduate certification of education. In D. Hopkins & K. Reid (Eds.), *Rethinking teacher education* (pp. 173–194). Kent, England: Croom Helm Ltd.

Haberman, M. (1982). Research on preservice laboratory and clinical experiences: Implications for teacher education. In Ken Howey (Ed.), *The education of teachers* (pp. 98–117). New York: Longman.

Hodges, C. (1982). Implementing methods: If you can't blame the cooperating teacher who can you blame? *Journal of Teacher Education, 33*(6), 25–29.

Joyce, B. R., & Showers, B. (1980). Improving inservice training: The message of research. *Educational Leadership, 37,* 279–385.

Kennedy, M. M. (1983). Working knowledge. *Knowledge: Creation, Diffusion, Utilization, 5,* 193–211.

Kennedy, M. M. (1987). Inexact sciences: Professional education and the development of expertise. In E. Rothkopf (Ed.), *Review of Research in Education, 13,* 133–167.

McIntyre, D. J., & Killian, J. E. (1986). Students' interactions with pupils and cooperating teachers in early field experiences. *The Teacher Educator, 22*(2), 2–9.

McNergney, R. F., & Francis, P. (1986). Clinical teacher development revisited. *Journal of Curriculum and Supervision, 1*(3), 197–204.

Schön, D. A. (1983). *The reflective practitioner.* New York: Basic Books.

Schön, D. A. (1987). *Educating the reflective practitioner.* San Francisco: Jossey Bass.

Tabachnik, B. R., Popkowitz, T. S., & Zeichner, K. M. (1979–80). Teacher education and the professional perspectives of student teachers. *Interchange, 10*(4), 12–29.

Tom, A. R. (1972). Selective supervision. *The Teacher Educator, 8,* 23–26.

Zeichner, K. M., & Liston, D. P. (1987). Teaching student teachers to reflect. *Harvard Educational Review, 57*(1), 23–48.

# 4 | Accountability for Professional Practice

## LINDA DARLING-HAMMOND

The issue of educational accountability is probably the most pressing and most problematic of any facing the public schools today. Gone are the days when a local town council hired the village schoolmaster and fired him at will for any cause. Gone, too, are the days when schoolteachers were so respected in their office that anything within the schoolroom walls was accepted as the rightful and unquestioned prerogative of school officials. A more highly educated populace has greater expectations of schools, and a more knowledge-oriented economy raises both the costs and benefits of school success or failure. Today, schools are being held to account by politicians, the general public, and parents for results they should be expected to produce and, often, for results over which they have little or no control.

In the current debates about accountability, cacaphony rules. There is little agreement, and perhaps even less clear thinking, about what accountability means, to whom it is owed, and how it can be operationalized. Many policy makers seem to equate accountability with something like the monitoring of student test scores, averaged for classrooms, schools, or school districts. Some believe that accountability can be enacted by statutes prescribing management procedures, tests, or curricula. Unfortunately, these approaches to accountability leave the student, the parent, the teacher, and the educational process entirely out of the equation. The production of a test score or a management scheme does not touch the issue of whether a student's educational interests are being well-served.

We need to begin to articulate what we mean by accountability, and in particular what we mean by professional accountability. I will hypothesize here that a meaningful system of accountability for public education should do three things.

1. *Set educationally meaningful and defensible standards* for what parents and members of the general public can rightfully expect of a school system, school, or teacher

2. *Establish reasonable and feasible means* by which these standards can be implemented and upheld
3. *Provide avenues for redress or corrections in practice* when these standards are not met, so that ultimately students are well-served

Given this framework, I will explore below how current systems of accountability are structured and how they would need to be changed to provide honest and useful vehicles for accountability in the context of schools intended to promote professional practice in teaching.

## MODELS OF ACCOUNTABILITY

Social transactions in our society are managed in a variety of ways, ultimately subject to democratic control. Through legislative bodies, the populace can decide whether an activity should be subject to governmental regulation and where that regulation should begin and end. When legislative government involvement has been eschewed or limited, control of an activity may revert, in whole or in part, to professional bodies, courts, or private individuals in their roles as clients, consumers, or citizens.

In any of these instances, accountability mechanisms are chosen to safeguard the public interest. These include at least the following:

- *Political accountability.* Elected officials must stand for re-election at regular intervals so that citizens can judge the representativeness of their views and the responsiveness of their decisions.
- *Legal accountability.* Courts must entertain complaints about violations of laws enacted by representatives of the public and of citizens' constitutionally granted rights, which may be threatened either by private action or by legislative action.
- *Bureaucratic accountability.* Agencies of government promulgate rules and regulations intended to assure citizens that public functions will be carried out in pursuit of public goals voiced through democratic or legal processes.
- *Professional accountability.* Governments may create professional bodies and structures to ensure competence and appropriate practice in occupations that serve the public, and may delegate certain decisions about occupational membership, standards, and practices to these bodies.
- *Market accountability.* Governments may choose to allow clients or consumers to select what services best meet their needs; to preserve the

utility of this form of accountability, monopolies are prevented, freedom of choice is protected, and truthful information is required of service providers.

All of these accountability mechanisms have their strengths and weaknesses, and each is more or less appropriate to certain types of activities. Political mechanisms can support the public establishment of general policy directions in areas subject to direct government control. Legal mechanisms are most useful when rights or proscriptions are clearly definable and when establishing the facts is all that is needed to trigger a remedy. Bureaucratic mechanisms are most appropriate when a standard set of practices or procedures can be easily linked to behavioral rules that will produce the desired outcomes. Market mechanisms are helpful when consumer preferences vary widely, when the state does not have a direct interest in controlling choice, and when government control would be counterproductive to innovation. Professional mechanisms are most important when safeguards for consumer choice are necessary to serve the public interest, but the technology of the work is uniquely determined by individual client needs and a complex and changing base of knowledge.

There are, of course, incentives in any of these systems for individuals to shirk their missions or for functional inadequacies to impair performance. (Public servants may use their position for private gain; courts may become overloaded; bureaucrats may fail to follow regulations; professionals may overlook incompetence; markets may break down due to regulatory or economic failures.) These problems can, presumably, be addressed by efforts to make the systems work more perfectly, often by overlaying another accountability mechanism against the first as a check and balance; for example, enacting an ethics-in-government law that adds legal accountability vehicles to the electoral process for governing the actions of public officials.

However, even when they function perfectly, any given mode of accountability has intrinsic limits, which must be weighed in the choice of which to use in varying circumstances. Electoral accountability does not allow citizens to judge each specific action of officials; nor does it necessarily secure the constitutional rights or preferences of citizens whose views and interests are in the minority. Legal accountability cannot be used in all instances: The reach of courts is limited to matters that can be legislated; not all citizens have access to courts; and courts are buffered from public opinion. Bureaucratic accountability does not guarantee results, but is concerned with procedures; it is effective only when procedures are known to produce the desired outcomes and when compliance is easily measured and secured. Professional accountability does not take public preferences into account; it responds to an authority outside the direct reach of citizens and may satisfy its purposes while ignoring competing public goals. Market accountability does not ensure citizens' access to services and relies on the spontaneous emergence of a variety of services to allow choice to operate as a safety valve for poor service provision.

Because of these intrinsic limits, no single form of accountability operates alone in any major area of public life. Hybrid forms are developed to provide checks and balances and to more carefully target vehicles for safeguarding the public interest toward the particular matters they can best address. The choices of accountability tools—and the balance among different forms of accountability—are constantly shifting as problems emerge, as social goals change, and as new circumstances arise.

## ACCOUNTABILITY IN EDUCATION

In education, it is easy to see that legal and bureaucratic forms of accountability have expanded their reach over the past 20 years, while electoral accountability has waxed and waned (with local and state school boards operating with reduced authority in some instances, and the purviews of elected and appointed officials shifting in many states). Market accountability is more often discussed as a possibly useful vehicle, but is still rarely used, except in a few districts that offer magnet schools or other schools of choice. Professional accountability is gaining in prominence as an idea for strengthening teaching quality, but it is as yet poorly defined and partially at odds with other forms of accountability currently in use.

### Bureaucratic Accountability

Bureaucratic organization and management of schools has increased since the early part of this century, when "scientific management" principles were first introduced into urban schools in an effort to standardize and rationalize the process of schooling. The view underlying this approach to managing schools is as follows: Schools are agents of government that can be administered by hierarchical decision making and controls.

Policies are made at the top of the system and handed down to administrators who translate them into rules and procedures. Teachers follow the rules and procedures (class schedules, curricula, textbooks, rules for promotion and assignment of students), and students are processed according to them.

This approach is intended to foster equal and uniform treatment of clients, and standardization of products or services, and to prevent arbitrary or capricious decision making. It works reasonably well when goals are agreed-upon and clearly definable, when procedures for meeting the goals can be specified, when the procedures are straightforward and feasible to implement, and when following these procedures is known to produce the desired outcomes in all cases. Bureaucratic accountability ensures that rules will be promulgated and compliance with them will be monitored. The promise that bureaucratic accountability mechanisms make is that violators of the rules will be apprehended, and consequences will be administered for noncompliance.

When bureaucratic forms are applied to the management of teaching, they rely on a number of assumptions.

- Students are sufficiently standardized that they will respond in identical and predictable ways to the "treatments" devised by policy makers and their principal agents.
- Sufficient knowledge of which treatments should be prescribed is both available and generalizable to all educational circumstances.
- This knowledge can be translated into standardized rules for practice; these can be operationalized through regulations and reporting and inspection systems.
- Administrators and teachers can and will faithfully implement the prescriptions for practice thus devised and transmitted to schools.

The circular bottom-line assumption is that this process, if efficiently administered, will produce the outcomes that the system desires. If the outcomes are not satisfactory, the final assumption is that the prescriptions are not yet sufficiently detailed or the process of implementation is not sufficiently exact. Thus, the solutions to educational problems always lie in more precise specification of educational or management processes.

In the bureaucratic model, teachers are viewed as functionaries rather than as well-trained and highly skilled professionals. Little investment is made in teacher preparation, induction, or professional development. Little credence is given to licensing or knowledge acquisition. Little time is afforded for joint planning or collegial consultation about problems of practice. Because practices are prescribed outside the school setting, there is no need and little use for professional knowledge and judgment. Thus, novice teachers assume the same responsibilities as 30-year veterans. Separated into egg-crate classrooms and isolated by packed teaching schedules, teachers rarely work or talk together about teaching practices. A rationale for these activities is absent from the bureaucratic perspective on teaching work.

In the bureaucratic conception of teaching, teachers do not need to be highly knowledgeable about learning theory and pedagogy, cognitive science and child development, curriculum and assessment; they do not need to be highly skilled, because presumably they do not make the major decisions about these matters. Curriculum planning is done by administrators and specialists; teachers are to implement a curriculum planned for them. Inspection of teachers' work is conducted by hierarchical superiors, whose job it is to ensure that the teachers are implementing the curriculum and procedures of the district. Teachers do not plan or evaluate their own work; they merely perform it.

Accountability is achieved by inspections and reporting systems intended to ensure that the rules and procedures are being followed. Teachers are held accountable for implementing curricular and testing policies, grading policies, assignment and promotion rules, and myriad other educational prescriptions, whether or not these "treatments" are appropriate in particular instances for particular students. As a consequence, teachers cannot be held accountable for meeting the needs of their students; they can only be held accountable for following standard operating procedures. The standard for accountability is compliance rather than effectiveness.

The problem with the bureaucratic solution to the accountability dilemma in education is that effective teaching is not routine, students are not passive, and questions of practice are not simple, predictable, or standardized. By its very nature, bureaucratic management is incapable of providing appropriate education for students who do not fit the mold on which all the prescriptions for practice are based.

## Public vs. Client Accountability

At present, I think it is fair to say that the use of legal and bureaucratic accountability mechanisms in education far outweighs the use of other forms, and that these mechanisms have overextended their reach for actually promoting positive practices and responsiveness to public and client needs. This statement should not be glossed over too lightly, though, for public and client needs are not identical, and positive practices are defined in the eye of the beholder. Indeed, there is a special tension in public education between the goals held by governments for public schools and the goals held by the clients of schools, for which different forms of accountability are needed. Because the needs, interests, and preferences of individual students and parents do not always converge with the needs, interests, and preferences of state or local governments, the question of accountability in education must always be prefaced by the questions "to whom?" and "for what?"

Public schools have been created primarily to meet the states' need for an educated citizenry. Indeed, public education is not so much a right accorded to students as an obligation to which they are compelled by law. State goals include

- Socialization to a common culture (education to meet social needs)
- Inculcation of basic democratic values and preparation of students to responsibly exercise their democratic rights and responsibilities (education to meet political needs)
- Preparation of students for further education, training, and occupational life (education to meet economic needs)

To meet these goals, a state further defines what type of socialization is desired, what manner of democratic preparation is to be given, and what forms of preparation—forms useful to the state's economic goals—are to be offered (Wise & Darling-Hammond, 1984).

Furthermore, the state has an interest in providing educational services both equitably (this state interest has sometimes had to be enforced by courts when it is ignored by legislators) and efficiently, so that taxpayers' burdens are not excessive or their tax monies wasted. Since equity and efficiency are difficult concepts to operationalize, they cause special accountability problems for bureaucrats and professionals to resolve. They also frequently stand in conflict with the needs and interests of individual students, as, for example, when "same" treatment does not produce appropriate treatment, or when "efficient" education does not produce quality education.

Individual consumers (parents and students) often hold different social, economic, and political goals than does the state government, and they very often disagree about how to pursue even commonly held goals. Furthermore, child-oriented definitions of student "needs" rarely match state definitions, since the former are unique to the individual child, and the latter are promulgated for all children in a state or for specified groups of children.

These definitions continually confront a tension that Thomas Green (1980) refers to as the dialectic between the "best" principle and the "equal" principle. The "best" principle is the proposition that each student is entitled to receive the education that is best for him or her; the "equal" principle is the proposition that each is entitled to receive an education at least as good as (equal to) that provided for others. In translation through legal or bureaucratic vehicles, "equal to" means "the same as," since these vehicles must operate by uniform standards. Efforts to individualize instruction through these vehicles invariably create groups of children, all of whom are then to be treated alike (hence, the tendency to create identifiable subsets of children, by age, grade level, measured ability, curriculum track, and so on). This may solve the state's problem of specifying inputs and desired outcomes, but it does not solve the student's or teacher's problem that children will still, come what may, fit untidily into the containers designed for them.

Thus, accountability for accomplishing state goals is a very different concept from accountability for accomplishing clients' goals. Indeed, accountability for meeting the needs of individual students is often in conflict—or at least in tension—with accountability for securing the public's preferences for education. Teachers and public school officials are the arbiters of these tensions. They strive to achieve a balance between meeting the state's goals and the needs of individual students. This requires a great deal of skill, sensitivity, and judgment, since the dilemmas posed by these two sets of goals are complex, idiosyncratic, and ever-changing.

Increasingly, though, attempts to provide public accountability have sought to standardize school and classroom procedures in the hopes of finding "one best system" by which all students may be educated. Codified by law, and specified more completely by regulation, these attempts have both "teacher-proofed" and "student-proofed" schooling, leaving little room for innovation or improvement of education. Indeed, this approach is criticized in recent reports as having created a situation in which "everyone has the brakes but no one has the motors" to make schools run well (Carnegie Forum, 1986).

Ironically, prescriptive policies created in the name of public accountability have begun to reduce schools' responsiveness to the needs of students and the desires of parents. In the cause of uniform treatment and in the absence of schooling alternatives, large numbers of students "fall through the cracks" when rules, routines, and standardized procedures prevent teachers from meeting students' individual needs. Those who can afford to do so leave for private schools. Those who cannot are frequently alienated and ill-served.

The theory underlying the press for teacher professionalism is that strengthening the structures and vehicles for creating and transmitting professional knowledge will prove a more effective means for meeting students' needs and improving the overall quality of education than will trying to prescribe educational practices from afar. This theory is based on a conception of teaching as complex, knowledge-based work requiring judgment in nonroutine situations and on a conception of learning as an interactive and individually determined process. These conceptions limit the applicability of legal and bureaucratic remedies for ensuring learning, by asserting the differential nature of effective interactions between teachers and learners, which is beyond the capacity of laws and regulations to predict or prescribe.

## Professional Accountability

Professionalism depends on the affirmation of three principles in the conduct and governance of an occupation.

1. Knowledge is the basis for permission to practice and for decisions that are made with respect to the unique needs of clients
2. The practitioner pledges his or her first concern to the welfare of the client
3. The profession assumes collective responsibility for the definition, transmittal, and enforcement of professional standards of practice and ethics

Professionals are obligated to do whatever is best for the client, not what is easiest or most expedient, or even what the client might want. They are also obligated to base a decision about what is best for the client on available knowledge—not just knowledge acquired from personal experience, but also clinical and research knowledge acquired by the occupation as a whole and represented in professional journals, certification standards, and specialty training. Finally, in fashioning their judgments about what strategies or treatments are appropriate, professionals are required to take into account the unique needs of individual clients.

These are fine goals, but how are they operationalized to result in something that might be called professional accountability? In policy terms, these requirements suggest greater regulation of *teachers*—ensuring their competence through more rigorous preparation, certification, selection, and evaluation—in exchange for the deregulation of *teaching*—fewer rules prescribing what is to be taught, when, and how. This is, in essence, the bargain that all professions make with society: For occupations that require discretion and judgment in meeting the unique needs of clients, the profession guarantees the competence of members in exchange for the privilege of professional control over work structure and standards of practice.

The theory behind this equation is that professional control improves both the quality of individual services and the level of knowledge in the profession as a whole. This occurs because decision making by well-trained professionals allows individual clients' needs to be met more precisely, and it promotes continual refinement and improvement in overall practice as effectiveness, rather than compliance, becomes the standard for judging competence.

It is important to note, too, that professional authority does not mean legitimizing the idiosyncratic or whimsical preferences of individual classroom teachers. Indeed, in other public service occupations, autonomy is the problem that professionalism is meant to address. It is precisely *because* practitioners operate autonomously that safeguards to protect the public interest are necessary. In occupations that have become professionalized, these safeguards have taken the form of screens to membership in the profession and ongoing peer review of practice. Collective autonomy from external regulation is achieved by the assumption of collective responsibility. Responsible self-governance requires, in turn, structures and vehicles by which the profession can define and transmit its knowledge base, control membership in the occupation, evaluate and refine its practices, and enforce norms of ethical practice.

In theory, then, teacher professionalism promises a more potent form of accountability for meeting students' needs than what courts and bureaucracies can concoct. It promises competence, an expanding knowledge base, concern for client welfare, and vehicles for enforcing these claims. In many respects, such accountability also serves the needs of the state by promoting better practice; but because professional accountability is explicitly *client-oriented* it will not fully represent the preferences of the general public. Hence, in working through a concept of professional accountability, we must keep in mind its limits for achieving public accountability as well as its promise.

## THE NATURE OF ACCOUNTABILITY IN PROFESSIONAL PRACTICE SCHOOLS

Professional practice schools have three missions with respect to accountability. First, they should model a professional form of accountability as it might ultimately be seen in all schools. Second, as induction centers, they implement a key accountability function for the profession as a whole. Third, as knowledge-producing institutions, they support and help to build the foundation on which professional accountability ultimately rests. These missions, as suggested by our earlier-stated criteria for accountability mechanisms, require that professional practice schools devote considerable attention to defining educationally meaningful *standards* of practice, creating reasonable *means* for upholding these standards, and establishing vehicles for *redress or corrections* of problems that arise.

The goals of professional accountability are to protect the public by ensuring that

1.  All individuals permitted to practice in certain capacities are adequately prepared to do so responsibly
2.  Where knowledge about practice exists, it will be used, and where certainty does not exist, practitioners will individually and collectively continually seek to discover the most responsible course of action
3.  Practitioners will pledge their first and primary commitment to the welfare of the client

The first of these goals—that *all* individuals permitted to practice are adequately prepared—is crucial to attaining the conditions for and benefits of professionalism. So long as anyone who is not fully prepared is admitted to an occupation where autonomous practice can jeopardize the safety of clients, the public's trust is violated. So long as no floor is enforced on the level of knowledge needed to teach, a professional culture in schools cannot long be maintained, for some practitioners will be granted control and autonomy who are not prepared to exercise it responsibly.

Professional practice schools serve a crucial function in the preparation of professional teachers. They are charged with completing the initial education of prospective teachers, by ensuring that they have the tools to apply theory in practice and by socializing them to professional norms and ethics. This mission requires (1) a conception of the understanding and capabilities to be acquired by novice teachers before they are allowed to practice autonomously; (2) means by which these understandings, including ethical and normative commitments, can be acquired with a high probability of success; and (3) safeguards to ensure that those sent forth from such schools are adequately prepared. In addition, as models of responsible professionalism, these schools must offer assurances to parents that their children will not be harmed by the (literal) practice of novices.

## A Conception of Teaching

In highly developed professions, the knowledge expected to be acquired in an apprenticeship or internship is decided by the profession through accrediting bodies that sanction such programs and through certification examinations that are taken after the induction experience has been completed. Until such time as these professional structures are available in education, though, professional practice schools will be at the forefront of defining what it is that a teacher needs to know to safely practice without intensive supervision.

In pragmatic terms, this is where the first knotty challenge facing such schools will arise. Although professionalism starts from the proposition that knowledge must inform practice, teacher education is often denounced and frequently avoided on the grounds that either it does not convey the knowledge necessary for real teaching (alternative certification plans argue this can be acquired on the job), or that there is no knowledge base for teaching anyway. Even trained and licensed teachers will come to their first teaching experiences with variable levels and types of knowledge, given the diversity of preparation experiences and the disparate standards for licensure both within and across states.

In wrestling with a conception of teaching knowledge, then, professional practice schools will form an implicit conception of their "curriculum" that must be based on assumptions—sure to be violated—about what novice teachers might already be expected to know. Even before they have begun, such schools will have to decide whether they will assume the mission of preparing, sometimes from "scratch," the unprepared, or whether they will develop some type of admissions standard that approximates a level of knowledge on which they feel they can successfully build. A possible middle ground is that the school will diagnose novices' knowledge at entry, requiring supplemental coursework in specific areas where a minimal understanding of rudiments of content or pedagogy has not yet been acquired.

This is more than an academic question, particularly for large city school systems that have many new entrants admitted on emergency or alternative certificates without prior teacher education, and others who are hired to teach in fields for which they have not had complete subject-matter preparation. The choices made in this regard will determine in many respects what methods of preparation and levels of responsibility will be suitable for novice teachers.

Many statements are possible about the kinds of understandings and capabilities professional practice schools should seek to exemplify and impart. Shulman (1987), for example, classifies the elements of teaching knowledge as follows:

• Content knowledge
• General pedagogical knowledge, with special reference to those broad

principles and strategies of classroom management and organization that appear to transcend subject matter

- Curriculum knowledge, with particular grasp of the materials and programs that serve as "tools of the trade" for teachers
- Pedagogical content knowledge, that special amalgam of content and pedagogy that is uniquely the province of teachers, their own special form of professional understanding
- Knowledge of learners and their characteristics
- Knowledge of educational contexts, ranging from the workings of the group or classroom, the governance and financing of school districts, to the character of communities and cultures
- Knowledge of educational ends, purposes, values, and their philosophical and historical grounds

To this list, I would add a grounding in professional ethics, so that teachers can responsibly resolve dilemmas of teaching practice. The goal, as Shulman (1987) puts it, "is not to indoctrinate or train teachers to behave in prescribed ways, but to educate teachers to reason soundly about their teaching as well as to perform skillfully" (p. 13).

Whatever the precise definition of knowledge that is arrived at, the professional practice school must have in mind what its expectations are for the understandings that undergird professional practice. It is on this basis that the school selects its staff, develops its program for induction, and assesses whether novices have been adequately prepared to practice autonomously.

### Structuring Professional Practice

The basic task here is constructing an organization that will seek, transmit, and use knowledge as a basis for teaching decisions; that will support inquiry and consultation; and that will maintain a primary concern for student welfare. Because knowledge is constantly expanding, problems of practice are complex, and ethical dilemmas result from conflict between legitimate goals, the establishment of professional norms cannot be satisfied by prescriptions for practice or unchanging rules of conduct. Instead, the transmission of these norms must be accomplished by socialization to a professional standard that incorporates continual learning, reflection, and concern with the multiple effects of one's actions on others as fundamental aspects of the professional role.

For a professional practice school, the accountability dilemmas associated with structuring practice are at least twofold.

1. How can the school guarantee that novices are given adequate preparation?
2. How can the school encourage the use of appropriate practices for all children it serves?

The induction mission of the school ought to warrant that those working with new teachers are themselves exemplars of good teaching; that the experiences of the new teachers will be structured to explicitly address the understandings they are expected to acquire; and that some means for assessing the progress of new teachers is used.

Faculty who are engaged in the induction of new teachers may or may not be all of the faculty employed in a professional practice school. If the school is to be an exemplar of good practice, certainly the entire staff must be committed to the tenets of professionalism and the goals of the school. Those who are specifically charged with the preparation of new teachers must themselves meet the standards of teaching knowledge and disposition toward which new teachers strive. This suggests that these faculty will be carefully selected for their capacities to teach adults as well as children. Selection should be conducted by other teaching professionals according to the standards defined earlier. If the school is to model professional accountability, selection by peers according to professional standards is a fundamental feature of the professionalization process.

What distinguishes the form of professional preparation envisioned here from the usual approaches to teacher induction is that, because a standard of practice is envisioned and articulated, haphazard or idiosyncratic training and experiences will be insufficient to guarantee that the standard has been met. Consequently, pairing of a beginning teacher with a mentor in a single class setting is not adequate to the task. The school must structure the experiences of beginning teachers so that they encounter a range of teaching situations and acquire a set of teaching and decision-making abilities. This suggests that the school has an explicit curriculum for beginning teachers composed of (1) formal instructional experiences, such as seminars, clinical conferences, readings, and observations of other teachers; and (2) clinical experiences in which the beginning teacher, under supervision, systematically encounters and examines the major domains of teaching knowledge.

To safeguard the welfare of students and facilitate the learning of novice teachers, beginning teachers should not have sole responsibility for a standard teaching load; they need to be given an appropriate and graduated degree of responsibility for teaching students and the opportunity to review major teaching decisions with expert faculty. Indeed, important decisions about students should not be made in isolation. The requirement for consultation is both a protection for students and a means of transmitting knowledge; it is also a means for socializing new teachers to norms of inquiry and collaboration.

In addition, beginning teachers should acquire experience with a variety of students and types of classes. To develop generalizable teaching skills and the ability to exercise judgment in diverse teaching situations, new teachers should learn to work with students at different cognitive stages and performance levels, from differing family backgrounds, and in different subject areas within the disciplinary or grade-level domain.

Finally, accountability for performing the training mission must be secured by assessing new teachers' progress toward the acquisition of professional knowledge and norms of conduct. Such assessment should be the basis for decisions about according additional responsibility for students to developing teachers and about "certifying" that novices are sufficiently prepared at the close of their experience to practice autonomously. At a minimum, this process should include frequent feedback to new teachers, establishment of opportunities to acquire those skills not yet adequately mastered, and consultation at regular intervals.

The conditions for responsible practice in a professional practice school obviously must include structures that promote inquiry and consultation among the faculty as a whole, not just those immediately engaged in supervising novices. Teacher isolation promotes idiosyncratic practice and works against the development and transmission of shared knowledge. Changing the egg-crate classroom structure and the groupings of students and teachers that maintain isolation will require major changes in teaching arrangements to promote team efforts and legitimize shared time. Many possibilities for reorganizing instruction, such as those pursued in the Coalition of Essential Schools (Sizer, 1988) and other similar initiatives (see, for example, Meier, 1987), can be considered. With respect to the accountability question, several features of school structure are particularly important.

1. The extent to which the organization of instruction fosters responsibility for individual students, that is, client-oriented accountability
2. The extent to which the school structure fosters the use of professional knowledge beyond that represented in the experiences of individual teachers

3. The extent to which the school structure supports continual self-evaluation and review of practice

Client-oriented accountability requires that teachers primarily teach *students* rather than teaching *courses,* that they attend more to learning than to covering a curriculum. If teachers are to be responsible for students and for learning, they must have sufficient opportunities to come to know students' minds, learning styles, and psychological dispositions, and they must be able to focus on student needs and progress as the benchmark for their activities. This seems obvious, but it is rendered improbable, if not impossible, as schools are now structured. The current structure ensures that specific courses and curricula will be offered and that students will pass through them, usually encountering different teachers from grade to grade and course to course, succeeding or failing as they may. This system does not offer accountability for student learning, only for the processing of students.

Client accountability entails at least two implications for the organization of schooling: that teachers will stay with students for longer periods of time (hours in the day and even years in the course of a school career) so that they may come to know what students' needs are, and that school problem solving will be organized around the individual and collective needs of students rather than around program definitions, grades, tracks, and labels.

Use of professional knowledge poses other requirements: that decision making be conducted on the basis of available *profession-wide* knowledge, not on the basis of individual proclivity or opinion, even collective opinion. When most schools do not even stock professional journals in their libraries, the challenge implied by this requirement is profound. In addition to shared time and expectations of consultation and collective decision making, vehicles must be found for teachers in professional practice schools to have access to the knowledge bases relevant to their work and to particular, immediate problems of teaching practice. Linkages to universities and access to professional development opportunities go part of the way toward solving this problem, but more is needed. Professional practice schools may need to create their own research teams to examine and augment available knowledge if practice is to be thus grounded.

Research in the professional practice school setting serves an important function for the development of knowledge, but it poses dangers as well. Experimentation can harm students, if it is conducted without care and appropriate safeguards. Too much innovation for its own sake can result in faddism and lack of a coherent philosophy over time and across classrooms in a school. Thus, research in the professional practice school must also be subject to careful faculty deliberation regarding its necessity, desirability, and likely effects on children; to monitoring while in progress; and to the informed consent of parents.

Finally, ongoing review of practice is central to the operation of professional organizations. This evaluative function serves the joint purposes of monitoring organizational activities and establishing a continual dialogue about problems of practice among the practitioners themselves. The very distant analog in school systems is program evaluation, an activity generally conducted by central office researchers who report findings to government sponsors and school board members. Teachers are neither the major producers nor consumers of such information. Hence, neither they nor their students are the major beneficiaries of such evaluation results.

Teachers must wrestle with and take responsibility for resolving immediate, concrete problems of teaching practice if teaching lore is ever to be transformed into meaningful professional standards. One could envision many methods for achieving this. Standing committees such as those used in hospitals could meet regularly to review practices in various subject areas or grade levels, or to examine other functional areas: academic progress; grading policies; student and teacher assignments to particular courses, programs, or teams; development of student responsibility; organization of instruction, and so on. Or more flexible approaches might be tried. Ad hoc research committees might be formed to examine particular problems, both as they manifest in the school and as they have been addressed by research. Faculty meetings could be used to investigate curricular strategies and other matters within and across departments or grade levels. What is critical is that teachers have both time to pursue these evaluations as part of their role (rather than as "released" or extracurricular time) and authority to make changes based on their collective discoveries.

One other point is worth making here: These evaluative and decision-making functions should be engaged in by all the teachers within the school, including the novices in training. Some proposals for "teacher leadership" envision a small cadre of lead teachers or master teachers who partake of administrative decision-making authority, while everyone else goes on about their work. The trickle-down theory of expertise does not presume a professional standard for all teachers; professional accountability does. Teachers will learn to weigh and balance considerations; to inquire, consult, and make collaborative decisions; to use and develop teaching knowledge to the extent that they are expected to do so. Socialization into these norms of inquiry and collaboration must be part of the preparation of beginning teachers and part of the daily life of all teachers if they are to begin to permeate the profession.

## Safeguards for Professional Practice

Even with all the professional accountability mechanisms described above, there are dangers that the needs of some students will not be diagnosed or fully met, that the concerns or preferences of parents will be inadequately attended to, that the continual juggling of multiple and competing goals will sometimes lose sight of some while seeking to secure others. Members of a profession, while setting their own standards, cannot seal themselves off too tightly from public scrutiny or from their clientele. When they do, they endanger their rights to self-governance, as other professions have discovered in recent years.

A number of means for providing safeguards and voice for clients and the public will have to be considered and shaped to fit the requirements for a professional practice school.

- Hierarchical regulation, which expresses the contract made between a state or district and its populace
- Personnel evaluation, which establishes avenues for ensuring faculty competence
- Participation and review procedures for parents, which create clear and meaningful avenues for expression of parents' views and concerns
- Reporting vehicles, which transmit the accomplishments of students in the school to parents and the general public

Standard practices in each of these areas are inadequate to provide genuine accountability. In many cases, standard practice also undermines professional practice. New contracts must be forged with states, districts, teacher associations, parents, and the public. A full exploration of the content of these new contracts is beyond the scope of this chapter, but the nature of the terrain is sketched briefly below.

The problems associated with hierarchical regulation of teaching have been articulated earlier. In school bureaucracies, authority for decisions and responsibility for practice are widely separated, usually by many layers of hierarchy. Boards and central administrators make decisions, while teachers, principals, and students are responsible for carrying them out. It is for this reason that accountability for results is hard to achieve. When the desired outcomes of hierarchically imposed policies are not realized, policy makers blame the school people responsible for implementation; practitioners blame their inability to devise or pursue better solutions on the constraints of policy. No one can be fully accountable for the results of practice when authority and responsibility are dispersed.

Yet policy makers have a responsibility to ensure fairness in the delivery of educational services; and district officials are liable for the actions of schools residing within their jurisdictions. Not all regulations can be dispensed with in the cause of professional practice. An heuristic is needed for sorting those regulations that must be observed from those that must be renegotiated or waived. As a first step, it is useful to divide responsibilities into those that must be centrally administered and those that, by their nature, cannot be effectively administered in a hierarchical fashion.

Wise (1979) offers a useful distinction between *equity* and *productivity* concerns. The former generally must be resolved by higher units of governance, since they

> arise out of the conflicting interests of majorities and minorities and of the powerful and powerless. Because local institutions are apparently the captives of majoritarian politics, they intentionally and unintentionally discriminate. Consequently, we must rely upon the policymaking system to solve problems of inequity in the operating educational system. (p. 206)

On the other hand, productivity questions cannot be solved by regulation, since the appropriate use of teaching knowledge is highly individualized, while policies are necessarily uniform and standardized. Thus, policy decisions about methods of teaching and schooling processes cannot ever meet the demands of varying school and student circumstances. These require renegotiation for the accommodation of professional practice.

Personnel evaluation, by this rubric, falls in the domain of professional determination. This could lead to its substantial improvement or to its avoidance and demise. This is a critical function of a profession, as the first promise a profession makes is oversight of competence to practice. The shortcomings of traditional evaluation practices and the outlines of more productive professional practices are described in detail elsewhere (see, for example, Darling-Hammond, 1986). In brief, these entail increased peer involvement in design and implementation of evaluation, and separation of the processes for encouraging professional learning from those for making personnel decisions (by committee and with attention to objectivity and due process safeguards). All of this is more easily said than done, however, and the resolution of issues regarding collective bargaining relationships, appropriate roles for administrators and teachers, and political turf battles will require courage and leadership from teachers.

Parent voice is particularly important and problematic for a professional practice school. In the first place, some parents will be uncomfortable with the unique qualities of the school. In addition, professional practice must be guided, to the extent possible, by knowledge, even where that conflicts with client preferences. On the other hand, best practice is never absolute or fully informed by research; it is a matter of judgment and frequently unique to the individual child, about whom the parent has substantial knowledge. The multiple goals of schooling will often stand in tension to one another. Parents must have a voice in determining the balance among goals, as they are compelled by the state to entrust their children to schools. Thus, parent voice must be secured in a fashion that few schools have yet managed.

The first requirement, I believe, is that professional practice schools must, for their clientele as well as their faculties, be schools of choice. No child should be compelled by neighborhood residence or other criterion to attend the school, although attendance should be open to those in the community who desire it. This both safeguards the rights of parents and students to voice their preferences for a form of education with which they feel comfortable and protects the school from the task of satisfying a clientele that might otherwise have widely differing and even opposing points of view. It also provides the school with information, legitimacy, and a form of external review. If schools of choice are chosen, they are legitimized; if they are not, self-examination is required.

Beyond choice, which is the easy part of the answer, parent voice can be fostered by (1) school structures for shared governance, (2) accessible review and appeals processes, and (3) parent involvement in decision making about individual children. Structures for shared governance, such as school–community councils, can provide a vehicle for the shared interests of the parent community to find legitimized and regular expression in the school context. Perhaps the most proactive form of shared governance among parents, teachers, and administrators is seen in Salt Lake City, where decision-making turf that is the joint domain of parents and faculty (e.g., the school schedule, discipline policies, and curricular emphases) is delegated to councils for determination by consensus and parity vote (see Wise, Darling-Hammond, McLaughlin, & Bernstein, 1984).

Mechanisms for review and appeal of specific concerns and complaints by a neutral third party supplement the shared governance mechanism, by providing a clear avenue for the resolution of individual problems. These mechanisms also provide information and external review for the school as a whole. Finally, the expectation that parents will be included in discussions of important decisions concerning their children prevents the insulation of the professional decision-making process from exposure to the real-world circumstances and concerns of families and communities.

The issue that most ties knots in discussions of accountability is the question of how individual and school expectations and accomplishments can be transmitted in an educationally productive manner to parents, students, and the public-at-large. Because school goals are numerous, diffuse, and difficult to quantify, simple statements of objectives and results can never completely capture what schools do or what their students accomplish. The counterproductive outcomes for instruction of mindlessly adopting simple performance measures, such as averages of student achievement test scores, have been well documented (see, for example, Haney & Madaus, 1986; Darling-Hammond & Wise, 1985). Though less discussed, even student grading mechanisms can work against student success. The assumptions behind grading schemes that students are to be ranked against each other and that their accomplishments can be captured in a single letter or number can trivialize the educational strivings of individual students and undermine their motivation and self-esteem, activating the Pygmalion principle rather than supporting learning.

Yet reporting vehicles serve an important accountability function by giving information to parents and policy makers about school practices and student progress. The press for such information is increasing and cannot be avoided. Professional practice schools must be at the forefront of efforts to devise educationally productive means for reporting what they and their students do. Untangling this knotty problem is well beyond the scope of this chapter. However, we can point to a few promising directions.

Recent emphasis in a few school restructuring efforts on "high-fidelity" representations of student accomplishments—demonstrations, exhibitions, and projects, for example—seeks more valid and less artificial tools for educational assessment. Narrative reports of student progress accompanied by cumulative portfolios can better represent what a student has learned than a letter grade can. Such results, by depicting the form of instruction as well, also better represent what the teacher and school have sought to accomplish. Much can be learned from the assessment systems of other countries, which stress these kinds of representations of learning as a means for both reporting outcomes and supporting meaningful and useful education (see, for example, Archbald & Newmann, 1988; Burstall, 1986; Educational Testing Service, 1988; Fong, 1987).

Ultimately, though, to satisfy the press for public accountability, entirely new means of reporting the aggregate accomplishments of students in a school will need to be developed. This puzzle is one that professional practice schools will undoubtedly encounter before they, or the profession, have developed an answer to it.

## A FOOTNOTE

Professional accountability seeks to support practices that are *client-oriented* and *knowledge-based*. It starts from the premise that parents, when they are compelled to send their child to a public school, have a right to expect that he or she will be under the care of competent people who are committed to using the best knowledge available to meet the individual needs of that child. This is a different form of accountability from that promised by legal and bureaucratic mechanisms, which ensure that when goals have been established, rules will be promulgated and enforced.

Professional accountability assumes that, since teaching work is too complex to be hierarchically prescribed and controlled, it must be structured so that practitioners can make responsible decisions, both individually and collectively. Accountability is provided by rigorous training and careful selection, serious and sustained internships for beginners, meaningful evaluation, opportunities for professional learning, and ongoing review of practice. By such means, professionals learn from each other, norms are established and transmitted, problems are exposed and tackled, parents' concerns are heard, and students' needs are better met.

In such a system, parents can expect that no teacher will be hired who has not had adequate training in how to teach, no teacher will be permitted to practice without supervision until he or she has mastered the professional knowledge base and its application, no teacher will be granted tenure who has not fully demonstrated his or her competence, and no decision about students will be made without adequate knowledge of good practice in light of students' needs. Establishing professional norms of operation, by the vehicles outlined above, creates as well a basis for parent input, and standards and methods for redress of unsuitable practice, none of which exist in a bureaucratic system of school administration.

This work is not easy, and it will not be accomplished quickly. As Clark and Meloy (1987) have noted,

> We counsel patience in the development of and experimentation with new organizational forms. We have been patient and forgiving of our extant

form. Remember that new forms will also be ideal forms. Do not press them immediately to their point of absurdity. Bureaucracy as an ideal form became tempered by adjectival distinctions—bounded, contingent, situational. New forms need to be granted the same exceptions as they are proposed and tested. No one seriously imagines a utopian alternative to bureaucracy. But realistic alternatives can be formed that consistently trade off control for freedom, the organization for the individual. And they can be built upon the principle of the consent of the governed. (p. 40)

This, in sum, is the challenge that faces professional practice schools.

## REFERENCES

Archbald, D. A., & Newmann, F. M. (1988). *Beyond standardized testing: Assessing achievement in the secondary school.* Reston, VA: National Association of Secondary School Principals.

Burstall, C. (1986, Spring). Innovative forms of assessment: A United Kingdom perspective. *Educational Measurement: Issues and Practice,* pp. 17–22.

Carnegie Forum on Education and the Economy. (1986). *A nation prepared: Teachers for the 21st century.* New York: Carnegie Corporation.

Clark, D. L., & Meloy, J. M. (1987, October). *Recanting bureaucracy: A democratic structure for leadership in schools.* Unpublished manuscript, University of Virginia, Charlottesville.

Darling-Hammond, L. (1986). A proposal for evaluation in the teaching profession. *Elementary School Journal, 86*(4), 1–21.

Darling-Hammond, L., & Wise, A. E. (1985). Beyond standardization: State standards and school improvement. *The Elementary School Journal, 85*(3), 315–336.

Educational Testing Service. (1988). *Assessment in the service of learning.* Princeton, NJ: Author.

Fong, B. (1987). *The external examiner approach to assessment.* Washington, DC: American Association for Higher Education.

Green, T. F. (1980). *Predicting the behavior of the educational system.* Syracuse, NY: Syracuse University Press.

Haney, W., & Madaus, G. (1986). *Effects of standardized testing and the future of the National Assessment of Educational Progress* (Working Paper for the NAEP Study Group). Chestnut Hill, MA: Boston College, Center for the Study of Testing, Evaluation and Educational Policy.

Meier, D. (1987, Fall). Success in East Harlem. *American Educator,* pp. 34–39.

Shulman, L. (1987). Knowledge and teaching: Foundations of the new reform. *Harvard Educational Review, 57*(1), 1–22.

Sizer, T. (1988). On changing secondary schools: A conversation with Ted Sizer. *Educational Leadership, 45*(5), 30–36.

Wise, A. E. (1979). *Legislated learning.* Berkeley: University of California Press.

Wise, A. E., & Darling-Hammond, L. (1984). Education by voucher: Private choice and the public interest. *Educational Theory, 34*(1), 29–47.

Wise, A. E., Darling-Hammond, L., McLaughlin, M. W., & Bernstein, H. T. (1984). The Salt Lake City (Utah) public school evaluation system. In *Case studies for teacher evaluation: A study of effective practices* (pp. 1–37). Santa Monica, CA: The RAND Corporation.

# 5 | Teacher Development in Professional Practice Schools

## ANN LIEBERMAN AND
## LYNNE MILLER

We approach the topic of teacher development in professional practice schools with both optimism and caution. We are optimistic because we think the time is ripe for the creation of professional practice schools and because we know from our own and others' experience that teacher development can improve teaching and schools. We are cautious because we also know that, in the name of professional development, educators have made mistakes. Too often, structured activities and programs have upheld the status quo rather than changed it, perpetuating the "paternalistic system that reinforces 'schooling as usual' " (Lambert, 1988, p. 666). Therefore, we define our use of the phrase *teacher development* and distinguish it from competing notions of inservice education and staff development.

To our way of thinking, the term *inservice education* has become synonymous with training and implies a deficit model of education. In the *National Society of Student Education Yearbook on Inservice* (Henry, 1957), contributors such as M. Miles and A. H. Passow focused on the technical aspects of teaching. After the launching of Sputnik, coincidentally the same year that the *Yearbook* was published, the idea of teacher inservice as remedial training took hold. Subject-matter specialists from the arts and science faculties in universities were enlisted to write "teacher-proof" curricula. Teacher institutes, funded under the National Defense and Educational Act (NDEA), proliferated. These institutes were designed either to train teachers to use new, externally developed instructional materials or to update teachers' academic thinking in the content areas. The many failures of this approach to professional development have been carefully documented (Sarason, 1982). One might suppose that the notion of inservice education as training died a quiet death some time ago. Sadly, this is not the case. In many districts and schools, professional development still implies a deficit training model. Assemblies filled with an entire school staff still dot the landscape of allocated "staff development days." Outside experts still transmit "the word" to the un-anointed, be it assertive discipline, mastery teaching, or the elements of effective schools. Teachers are viewed as "the passive recipients of some-one else's knowledge" (Miller, in press), rather than as sources of knowl-edge themselves or as active participants in their own growth and devel-opment.

The term *staff development*, on the other hand, implies a broader notion of professional growth—one with which we are more, but not totally, comfortable. In the mid-1970s, a major shift in the research on and writing about staff development took place, exemplified by the find-ings of the Rand Change Agent Study (McLaughlin & Marsh, 1979), Goodlad's analysis of the League of Cooperating Schools (1975), and Hall and Loucks's work on teacher concerns (1979). This shift is most notable for its emphasis on the school as an organization and the connec-tion that it makes between the development of teachers as individuals and the development of the school as a whole. Over a decade ago, we defined staff development as "working with at least a portion of a staff over a period of time with the necessary supportive conditions" (Lieberman & Miller, 1979, p. ix). While this approach to teacher development was more broadly construed than inservice training, it often, though not al-ways, assumed that the role of development was to assist teachers in either adopting an externally designed program, making adaptations to some technological innovations, or implementing a federal or state pro-gram.

We will therefore use the words *teacher development* when we write and talk about professional growth activities in a professional practice school. By teacher development, we mean continuous inquiry into prac-tice. In terms of professional development, we see the teacher as a "reflec-tive practitioner" (Schön, 1983, 1987), someone who has a "tacit knowl-edge base" and who then builds on that knowledge base through ongoing inquiry and analysis, continually rethinking and re-evaluating values and practices. Teacher development is not only the renewal of teaching, but also the renewal of schools. Teacher development is, in effect, culture building. In the following pages, we first provide a framework for devel-oping a culture of inquiry in a school; then we consider professional growth activities appropriate to that culture; and finally we discuss some of the problems and dilemmas that must be recognized and worked through to maintain and support teacher development in professional practice schools.

## BUILDING A CULTURE OF SUPPORT FOR
## TEACHER INQUIRY

Having made the case for teacher development as continuous inquiry into practice, we are well aware of the complexity of this notion, the difficulty of transforming it into reality, and the necessity of having, or creating, a culture in the school that supports teachers as they become active inquirers into the process of teaching and learning. Fortunately, in the last few years, research and practice have provided some important insights about how to constitute such a culture. Five elements have emerged as essential.

1. Norms of colleagueship, openness, and trust
2. Opportunities and time for disciplined inquiry
3. Teacher learning of content in context
4. Reconstruction of leadership roles
5. Networks, collaborations, and coalitions

Combined, they create a culture of support for teachers engaged in continuous inquiry.

### Colleagueship, Openness, and Trust

Little (1981, 1986), in what has become a benchmark study on staff development, followed six urban schools as they became involved in district-sponsored staff development. Her findings indicate that norms of colleagueship and experimentation are most responsible for the successful implementation of new programs. In schools where the principal actively engaged with teachers and announced expectations for and modeled behaviors of colleagueship, there was increased support for self-examination, risk-taking, and collective reflection on practice. When teachers and principals observed each other in classrooms, had time to talk about what they were doing, and worked to find solutions for commonly defined problems, the life of the teachers in the school improved. Traditions of privacy, practicality, and isolation (Lieberman & Miller, 1984) were replaced by shared ownership of issues, a willingness to consider alternative explanations for practices and behaviors, and a desire to work together as colleagues. In effect, in creating an innovative staff development organization to support a new program, the staff was building a new culture for the school and defining new ways of being for themselves as teachers. As Little (1986) writes,

The successful program rested on long-term habits of shared work and shared problem solving among teachers. Such patterns of mutual assistance, together with mechanisms by which teachers can emerge as leaders on matters of curriculum and instruction, are also typical. (p. 42)

These notions of shared work, shared problem solving, mutual assistance, and teacher leadership in curriculum and instruction are—to our mind—the cornerstones of a school culture that supports continuous inquiry into practice.

Rosenholtz (1989), in her study of the school as a workplace, adds to our understanding of the effects of the norms Little describes. Rosenholtz categorizes schools as either "learning-enriched" or "learning-impoverished." Learning-enriched schools had collaborative goals at the building level, minimum uncertainty, positive teacher attitudes, principal support of teachers to the point of removing barriers, and support for collaboration rather than completion. On the other hand, in learning-impoverished schools there were no clear or shared values, teachers rarely talked to each other, work was perceived as routine, and both self-reliance and isolation flourished. In the learning-impoverished schools, teachers, with no vehicle for discussion or shared reflection, retreated to their individual classrooms, kept quiet about their successes and failures, and—afraid of being found inadequate—assumed a public stance as experts. In the learning-enriched schools, where teachers shared their successes and failures, they were more willing to identify and explore common problems and seek common solutions. The myth of expertise was replaced by the reality of collective struggle and discovery. Like Little, Rosenholtz provides evidence that colleagueship and collaboration provide some of the necessary conditions for teachers to reconceptualize their work, to engage in active investigations about their practices, and to expect that professional learning and growth are part of their work life in schools.

## Opportunities and Time for Disciplined Inquiry

In a school where teachers assume leadership in curriculum and instruction and where reflective action replaces routinized practice, providing opportunities and time for disciplined inquiry into teaching and learning becomes crucial. Unlike traditional school settings, professional practice schools are places where teachers, sometimes working with university scholars and sometimes working alone, do research on, by, and for themselves. Professional practice schools must provide the conditions that allow teachers to develop the skills, perspective, and confidence to do their own systematic investigation.

The notion of teacher-as-researcher is not new. Writing over 20 years ago, Schaefer (1967), then dean at Teachers College, Columbia University, urged that schools should organize as "centers of inquiry." More recently, Myers (1989), then president of the California Federation of Teachers and now executive director of the National Council of Teachers of English, argued that "school site teacher-research projects are a basic requirement of the current second wave of school reform" (p. 1). The case, then, has been made for teacher research, but the question remains: How do schools organize themselves and create the necessary conditions so that teacher research is encouraged, supported, and used?

The answer, we suspect, is not to hold externally driven workshops on research methods and then ask school staffs to apply the findings to classroom practice. Rather, the research sensibility must be infused into the daily life and work of the school. Such an infusion takes time and commitment. It begins with an acknowledgment of the importance of norms of colleagueship and experimentation; it builds on shared problem identification and a mutual search for solutions; it depends on taking a risk in the classroom; and it requires the support of colleagues. Let us present a case in point.

Mary George is a first-grade teacher in a school trying to organize itself around Schaefer's (1967) notion of schools as centers of inquiry. For over a year, she and her colleagues have been meeting in grade-level teams and in school-wide forums. The question with which the faculty has been grappling over the years is, "How do we understand more about how children learn?" Mary has had no formal training in research. What she does have is a very specific problem that has been troubling her and other teachers for some time. Namely, how do children approach the new words they encounter in their reading? Like her colleagues, Mary has been torn between phonics and whole language approaches but has been wary about accepting one to the exclusion of the other. She and her problem go into class one day, and when she generates a list of words that students miss in an initial reading of a "big book," she begins a spontaneous inquiry into how children learn new words. She asks the children, "How many of you could figure out the word *left?*" One boy raises his hand and explains how he sounded out the word, beginning with the initial consonant and moving on to the vowel and the final consonant sounds. Raising hers, a girl begins to explain that she knew the story was about hands, and she knew that people have left and right hands, and she knew that the word in question began with *l,* so she figured out that the word must be *left*. A third child, another girl, her hand also raised, tells the class that she knew the word because she saw it in another book. She proudly finds the other book in the classroom library and shows it to the class.

This simple experiment that Mary George conducted in her classroom was, actually, the beginning of research. Mary acknowledged later, in discussing with her colleagues what she did in class, that she considered her initial question an enormous risk. Though she had never approached her teaching as research before, she acknowledged that the ethos of inquiry that dominated the school and the support she knew she would get from her colleagues gave her the courage to risk her experiment. She was delighted with the results, as were the rest of the first-grade teachers, who each took Mary's question to her next class. Together, the first-grade teachers began putting together the pieces of the puzzle of word recognition in a way that made sense to them and had value for their classroom practices. Perhaps it can be shared eventually with other teachers through presentations at conferences, in published papers, or through electronic networks, and thus help teachers in other schools.

Teacher research can be more complex and more sophisticated than Mary George's spontaneous inquiry. But we should not let sophistication and complexity become the criteria by which we judge disciplined inquiry into practice. Rather, the importance of the question, the legitimacy of the sources of data, and the usefulness of the results should guide our practice. What is important is that authentic teacher research develops in an environment where culture building and professional colleagueship are also being nurtured and sustained.

## Teacher Learning of Content in Context

One may argue that all of this talk about teacher development as continuous inquiry into practice is long on process and short on content, that it places too much value on reflection and sharing and not enough value on what is being reflected upon and what is being shared. As Cooper (1988) reminds us, "In professional settings, when teachers are moved to share, it is usually because they are proud of something they have done with children" (p. 51). At the present moment, we think there is reason to be proud of what we call content-in-context learning, reason to share these approaches, and reason to make them the centerpiece of curriculum and instruction in professional practice schools.

Unlike the call for "cultural literacy" and "core learnings," the movement for content-in-context learning acknowledges the complexity of the educational enterprise without relinquishing the mission that educators have to teach children something of enduring value. Central to this school of thought is the notion that students come to school with a wealth of prior knowledge and ongoing access to experience that can be tapped to motivate and ground school learning. As our discussion unfolds, it should become obvious why this approach to instruction is so compatible with teacher development as we've defined it. There are many examples of content-in-context learning, including the writing process approach, whole language learning, math through manipulation, hands-on science, and "the Foxfire approach" (Wigginton, 1989).

These approaches to instruction both engage teachers in focusing on student-oriented learning and change the ground rules for teacher learning and development. What distinguishes these approaches to curriculum and instruction from the curricular reforms of past movements is their focus not only on student motivation and student-centered curricula but also increasingly on the facilitative role of the teacher. These approaches offer practical examples of how to act on the new understandings emerging from recent research on cognition. Insights such as those recognizing the need to provide problem-solving activities and the fact that solving problems requires a mix of social and cognitive skills, along with research that indicates that students need different modes of instruction (some need loose structures to invent; others need direct instruction before they can learn under conditions of structural looseness), are helping to inform new curricular and instructional demands on teachers (Devaney & Sykes, 1988).

One example of the change in ways teachers learn in practice is being carried out by Wigginton through Foxfire. Foxfire, much more than a publication, is a style of education best characterized as having the following ingredients (Wigginton, 1989):

- All work that teachers and students do together must flow from student desire.
- Connections of the work to the surrounding community and the real world outside the classroom are clear.
- The work is characterized by student action rather than passive reception of processed information.
- A constant feature of the process is its emphasis on peer teaching, small group work, and teamwork.
- The role of the teacher is that of collaborator and team leader and guide, rather than boss or the repository of all knowledge.
- There must be an audience beyond the teacher for student work.
- The academic integrity of the work must be absolutely clear.
- The work must include honest evaluation of skills and/or content.

- As the year progresses, new activities should grow out of the old. As the students become more thoughtful participants in their own education, the goal must be to help them become increasingly able and willing to guide their own learning, fearlessly, for the rest of their lives.

We think these nine "ingredients" incorporate many of the principles of curriculum and instruction implied in contemporary research on cognition. We also believe that this style of education happens best in an environment that values openness and collaboration and encourages disciplined inquiry. If professional practice schools are, in fact, centers of inquiry, where continuous teacher development is the norm, then the content-in-context style of education provides much of the substance around which inquiry may be focused. But, as we cautioned earlier, experimenters must continuously examine these process approaches to student learning and teacher facilitation. If the approach is working, students' products must grow in complexity and thought. For example, student writing should include extensive revision, during which process clarity should improve and better images should deepen. A process approach should, eventually, engage students in thinking critically, writing better, and moving beyond subjects like "What I did on my summer vacation." Better process does not automatically mean better products. Both process and products must be scrutinized by teachers and students for their significance, depth, and enhanced understanding. We are talking not about panaceas but about development of "habits of mind" that make it legitimate to continually ask questions of practice.

## Reconstruction of Leadership Roles

In traditional school settings, leadership is defined by one's position in the organization. Principals lead; teachers do not. In professional practice schools, the whole concept of leadership is being reconstructed. Sergiovanni (1987) makes what we think is a useful distinction between technical and managerial conceptions of leadership and cultural leadership. He writes,

> In human enterprises such as the profession of teaching and schooling, technical and managerial conceptions should always be subordinate to human needs and actions and should always be practiced in service of human ends. Cultural leadership—by accepting the realities of the human spirit, by emphasizing the importance of meaning and significance, and by acknowledging the concept of professional freedom linked to values and norms that make up a moral order—comes closer to the point of leadership. (p. 127)

Sergiovanni is proposing that principals learn to think and act as leaders in ways different from those of custom and tradition. According to Sergiovanni, leaders lead by purpose and empowerment, exercising power but of a different sort than usually practiced. Theirs is "power to accomplish" rather than "power over people and events." They practice the concept of "leadership density . . . the extent to which leadership roles are shared and the extent to which leadership is broadly exercised" (p. 122). When so construed, leadership, something that both administrators and teachers have and use, becomes an essential ingredient in transforming schools into centers of inquiry.

For principals, life in such a setting requires a radical shift in attitudes and behaviors. In a compelling study of two high school principals, Derrington (1989) brings home the difficulty building administrators have in making the transition from technical and managerial leadership to cultural leadership. In the transition, he identifies three major steps with subsets, as shown in Table 5.1.

For teachers, it is equally difficult to assume new roles. Wasley (1989) uncovers many of the tensions and dilemmas that teacher leaders face as they assume new roles in schools. She notes that all the teacher leaders she studied felt constrained by time—time to both teach and lead effectively and time to work collaboratively with their colleagues. Teacher leaders were often confused about the primary purpose of their positions; were they to support teachers or were they to support administrators? In addition, they had a difficult time dealing with their colleagues in their new leadership roles. The egalitarian ethic dominates teaching, and many teachers have difficulty recognizing one of their own as a leader. To para-

**Table 5.1 The role of the principal: Tradition, transition, and transformation**

| Tradition | Transition | Transformation |
|---|---|---|
| The boss | The Lone Ranger | Parallel leadership |
| Branch manager | Hero | Hero maker |
| Adversarial | Competitve | Collegial |
| Views teachers as objectives for improvement | Views teachers as vehicles for improvement | Views teachers as partners for improvement |
| Works through directive | Works through small groups | Works through collaboration and power equalization |
| Rewards and punishes | Builds coalitions | Solves problems |

*Source:* Derrington, 1989, p. 180

phrase George Orwell's epigram, the notion that all teachers are equal but some teachers are more equal than others goes against the grain. Most important, the success of teacher leadership depended on the principal's ability to make the transition from traditional to transformative or cultural leadership.

It is clear, then, that one of the tasks a professional practice school faces is to make the transition from bureaucratic and hierarchical modes of leadership to alternative forms. That this process is difficult and fraught with tension must be acknowledged. What also must be acknowledged is that in schools where principals and teachers together make the transition, there exists the real possibility for colleagueship, collaboration, and the development of a new and fruitful professional culture. In schools where teachers are making responsible, well-grounded decisions about instruction in their classrooms and where principals are supportive of those decisions, the possibility for continuous learning takes root. One such example shows what this could look like. Soo Hoo (1989) describes a collaborative project in which she, in collaboration with another principal and a university faculty member, engaged teachers in a discussion of the misuses of standardized tests. Teachers generated such questions expressing their concern as

- How do we know students are learning?
- How do we capture the data available in our classrooms?
- What are some new ways of displaying student achievement?

Teachers kept journals, while the university researcher made observations and helped with additional data-collection techniques (Kerchner, 1989). Through monthly meetings and discussions about the information teachers collected and used, as well as about alternative sources of data, the principal helped a culture of inquiry develop. In this case the principal, teachers, and university researcher provided the group with the impetus to examine the frustrations of testing and free a variety of understandings about assessment, which in turn led to other subjects for inquiry. Again, the description and practice begin to show us how to think about and engage teachers.

## Networks, Collaborations, and Coalitions

While it is important to concentrate energies on the specific school site, support systems outside the school also need to be developed. Too often schools in the process of radical transformation suffer from the "funny farm syndrome" (Goodlad, 1988). They stand out in their district as different and therefore often threatening. Teachers involved in professional practice schools may find that it is difficult to explain to colleagues within their own district just what they're about and that the support they need from the immediate environment is missing. Forming networks, collaborating, and creating or joining coalitions can combat the "funny farm syndrome" in providing support and encouragement for teachers who continue to experiment, to question, and to work to change common practices in an effort to improve education for children.

Networks, collaborations, and coalitions take many forms. They may be informal collections of people, or they may be more formalized partnerships among institutions. In any case, such groupings share some common characteristics. They are alternative in nature, share a common purpose, exchange information and psychological support, are voluntary, and are based on equal participation of all members (Parker, 1979).

The Puget Sound Educational Consortium and the Southern Maine Partnership are both members of the National Network for Educational Renewal, a national coalition of school/university partnerships. In both Washington and Maine, the partnerships serve more to connect people across schools and districts than to connect schools to the university. In both settings, groups of teachers come together regularly to discuss and act on matters of common concern. In the past 2 years, groups of teachers have dealt with issues of equity, teachers' leadership, restructuring schools, grouping practices, early childhood education, and at-risk students. The groups' power stems from the fact that they are self-directed, define their own agendas, and provide the opportunity for teachers of like mind and like disposition to exchange experiences and ideas in an atmosphere of support and common understanding. People involved claim that group participation provides the support they need to return to their schools with renewed energy and commitment.

The Coalition of Essential Schools is an example of collaboration at the national level, where schools are drawn together by a common purpose and a clearly defined mission. The Coalition grew out of the work of Ted Sizer (1984) and comprises over 40 high schools that ascribe to a set of principles that involve different roles for teachers as generalists and students as workers, and a different conception of the school curriculum; "less is more" has become the credo of the group. Though the Coalition does not provide much opportunity for face-to-face interaction among teachers at member schools, it does serve as a source of support for schools, many of which are isolated in their districts and look to a national movement to help legitimate their local efforts.

The American Federation of Teachers Center for Restructuring also helps teachers, schools, and school districts involved in restructuring, through networks of common interest, publication of a bimonthly newsletter, *Radius,* and conferences and meetings on subjects of common concern. A leadership network, the Urban District Leadership Consortium, brings together superintendents, school board members, and union presidents of districts involved in education reform.

Networks, collaborations, and coalitions need not be as formal as those we've discussed here. Through the Philadelphia Teachers Learning Cooperative (Buchanan et al., 1984), teachers come together on an informal basis once a month to discuss preassigned reading. In other cities and towns, teachers have joined to form small resource centers where they can meet to discuss issues, exchange ideas, learn about effective practices, and develop learning materials.

Whole schools, like individual teachers, can become isolated and estranged from the mainstream. Both must reach out beyond traditional borders and create sources of support, challenge, and legitimacy. Teachers who see themselves as part of a school in the process of change must also see themselves as part of a profession in the process of change. In that way, the norms and values of the school become part of a larger social system, one that sustains and encourages improvement.

## TEACHER DEVELOPMENT IN PROFESSIONAL PRACTICE SCHOOLS

The five elements that combine to create a culture of support for teacher inquiry do not take root quickly. It takes time for change to happen, even in a school that defines itself as different. Teacher development activities must occur alongside the development of the new school culture. In fact, teacher culture and development are part of the same process in a professional practice school. This means that activities for teacher development are

- Designed around notions of colleagueship, openness, and trust
- Provide time and space for disciplined inquiry
- Focus on teacher learning of content in context
- Provide opportunities that lead to new leadership roles
- Lead to networking activities and coalition building beyond the boundaries of the school

Several examples of activities for teacher development that seem to combine these elements and hold particular promise for professional practice schools follow.

**Teacher study groups.** Such groups meet regularly to discuss an agreed-upon topic or theme. Teachers rotate leadership of the group. The role of the designated teacher leader is to select a common reading and make it available to all group members before the meeting, to structure discussion by preparing a question or problem to answer, to facilitate discussion, to ensure that minutes of the meeting are taken and distributed, and finally to guide the group in making a decision about the direction the next meeting should take. In general, teacher study groups take place outside the school in an informal setting around a potluck meal or similar occasion to eat together.

**Curriculum writing.** Groups of teachers work together over time with the intention of developing an instructional program for use in the classroom. The product varies as the task varies and may take the form of a guide for teaching, an inventory of classroom practices, a statement of expectations of learners and teachers, a program evaluation, a set of recommendations for program design—anything that meets the needs, interests, and inventiveness of the teachers involved (Miller, in press). Teachers initiate and lead curriculum writing groups, which function as long as it takes to complete a task, allowing teachers the opportunity to move in and out of groups as time and interest permit.

**Teacher research projects.** Such projects may be individually or group initiated. The project begins with the identification of a problem that matters to someone. Even though one person's problem may seem trivial to someone else, it is important to assume that each individual or group engaged in research has a legitimate concern that needs to be addressed. The goal of the research is both to understand practice and to improve it. The majority activity of teacher research is the collection and analysis of data. Data collection need not be cumbersome or overly technical. Data can be collected through observation, informal interviewing, journal entries, and brief surveys. Researchers do not have to worry about doing complex statistical analyses or proving the generalizability of findings, since the problem under consideration is usually idiosyncratic to the people involved or to the specific school. Often, teacher research is published informally for the information and use of other faculty members.

**Peer observation.** Teachers, usually in pairs, make informal contracts to visit each other's classroom and observe each other's teaching. Sometimes, the visitor concentrates on the behaviors and practices of the teacher being observed. At other times, the visiting teacher focuses on the actions of the students or of one or two students in particular. In any event, the purpose of the observation is mutually determined before the visit takes place. Afterward, the visitor and the observed teacher take time to discuss what happened. It is the role of the visiting teacher to provide descriptive feedback to the practicing teacher, and it is the role of the observed teacher to make sense of the feedback, either alone or in consultation with the visiting teacher. The contract, renegotiated after each visit, may be altered or terminated at any mutually agreed-upon point.

**Case conferences.** These meetings engage teachers in a method of problem solving usually reserved for medical personnel and social workers. In the case conference, a group of teachers agree to meet to discuss individual students. The person presenting the case is responsible for developing a history of the child in school, a description of behaviors, attitudes, or academic concerns. The task of the other group members is to pose questions that help clarify the issues at hand and to offer suggestions for solving problems. Each meeting focuses exclusively on one case, and participants rotate in presenting cases to the group.

**Program evaluation and documentation.** Teachers want to evaluate current practices as part of an ongoing investigation of what works and what doesn't work for children. As new programs are put in place, new textbooks adopted, new practices of grouping students initiated, new approaches to instruction implemented, and alternative modes of assessment designed, teachers can collect information useful for future decision making. Using the techniques of teachers' research, an evaluation team collects data on a program or approach that the faculty as a whole has decided is worth investigating. The evaluation team analyzes the data and presents its findings to the faculty for consideration and action. The role of the evaluation team is not to judge effectiveness, but rather to collect data for decision making by the larger faculty.

**Trying out new practices.** Experimenting with innovative techniques, with systematic support from colleagues, is one way to make it easier for teachers to try and fail and try again, without quick retreats to routine, safe ways of doing things. As teachers become interested in content-in-context learning approaches, they may want to experiment with process writing, begin a Foxfire project, or incorporate experiential learning activities into their teaching. We have found that the closer change gets to the individual classroom, the riskier it gets. When a cadre of teachers decides to try out something together, it is easier to experiment and take risks (Little, 1986). One such group follows a pattern in which teachers

- Commit to implement a new approach
- Agree to meet regularly to discuss what is happening to them personally in their classrooms
- Contract to observe each other and to provide feedback on the new practice
- Agree to suspend all judgment and evaluation of themselves and others
- Work together to become comfortable with what they are doing and to support each other in doing it better
- Give themselves ample time to try and fail and try and succeed

In the end, teachers become confident about new practices and make decisions about whether to incorporate them into their existing repertoire, to modify them to suit individual needs, or to reject them as not helpful in improving their teaching.

**Teacher resource centers.** Such centers can be easily structured within a school. A small room off the library or media center, a converted stockroom, a renovated space hidden somewhere in the building—all suffice. We have seen teachers' resource rooms in the basements of buildings, even in old rest rooms. The place doesn't matter; what matters is that a place exists where teachers come together in the school to read journals, view educational videos, peruse books and catalogs, or simply engage in informal, professional conversation. We suspect, however, that even in a professional practice school there will still be a need for a traditional teachers' lounge, where staff can banter and gripe as an antidote to the tensions that come with teaching. The teacher resource room, then, serves as an alternative to the lounge, with alternative norms, expectations, and interaction among colleagues during the school day.

**Participation in outside events and organizations.** Teachers can make connections outside the boundaries of the school where they work every day through joining out-of-school groups and activities. Provision for teachers to visit other schools that are engaged in reform and restructuring efforts is a valuable way for broadening perspectives, becoming energetic, and considering new ideas. When teachers are actually practicing new approaches or subjects and have already had some success, opportunities to teach others about how they have learned become another powerful means of professional development. Attendance at regional conferences is still another way that teachers can reach out and connect with kindred spirits in schools. Participation in partnerships with universities and business, involvement in coalitions with other agencies, and membership in a formal network of teachers or schools are yet other avenues for growth and development.

In this partial listing of the kinds of teachers' development activities possible as part of the general organization of a professional practice school, we emphasize that none of the approaches we suggest is an "add on"; none is initiated outside the work life concerns of teachers; none is designed for teachers by others. Each teacher contributes to the development of a new school culture; each acknowledges that the major goal of teacher development is continuous inquiry into practice.

## TEACHER DEVELOPMENT: CHANGING STUDENT AND ADULT WORKING CONDITIONS

Our view of teacher development ends where it began, with the recognition that engaging teachers in creating professional practice schools cannot be isolated from the larger vision of designing schools that work for all students. This means that the entire school becomes involved in discussion and action around the issues of teaching and learning, such as uncovering new knowledge about how students learn, understanding diverse multicultural populations of students, as well as developing sensitivities to changing cultural contexts—all concerns that call for new ways of thinking about and organizing teaching to enable students to participate in their own learning.

Teachers, long engaged in successful and unsuccessful private struggles with their students, need to create and work in structures that are both collective and collaborative. The isolated classroom must give way to genuine colleagueship, just as the insulated school must expand to include the whole community. This means that the workplace for both students and adults must change, for they are intimately connected with each other. We know that teacher development involves teachers in learning about how to work together, how to make collective decisions, and how to structure continuous opportunities for their own growth. But at the same time, teachers must be constantly involved in new learning about students—their motivation, engagement, connection, and experience—through practicing new ways of teaching and providing for new ways of student learning. These two strands represent two distinct parts of teacher development, each part taking time, energy, and new knowledge.

We are cautious about predicting that positive changes in the adult workplace will lead to positive changes in the students' learning environment, or the other way around. *The two environments connect only if explicit connections are made.* It is possible for teachers to participate on school site committees, to be more actively involved in decision making, and to deal with conflict and negotiate contracts for greater teacher participation in the running of a school, *without* changing what goes on in classrooms. And conversely, it is possible for several teachers to run classrooms characterized by cooperative-learning teams, student-centered learning, and a focus on problem-solving activities, *without* addressing the need for school-wide structures that promote collegiality and continuous inquiry, which in turn support efforts to improve learning for students.

We are optimistic, however, that what happens to students, teachers, and schools will not happen in isolation, because professional practice schools can indeed value, promote, organize, and practice teacher development by explicitly connecting it to student development. Professional practice schools can provide a variety of learning environments where students can be active learners and a workplace for the teachers and other staff, rich in continuous inquiry, peer discussion, and increased opportunities for adult learning.

## REFERENCES

Buchanan, J., Edelsky, C., Kanevsky, R., Klausner, E., Lieberman, G., Mintier, J., Mantoya, B., Morris, E., Striebe, L., & Wice, B. (1984). On becoming teacher experts: Buying time. *Language Arts, 61*(7), 731–736.

Cooper, M. (1988). Whose culture is it, anyway? In A. Lieberman (Ed.), *Building a professional culture in schools* (pp. 44–54). New York: Teachers College Press.

Derrington, M. (1989). *The role of the principal: Tradition, transition, and transformation.* Unpublished doctoral dissertation, University of Washington.

Devaney, K., & Sykes, G. (1988). Making the case for professionalism. In A. Lieberman (Ed.), *Building a professional culture in schools* (pp. 3–22). New York: Teachers College Press.

Goodlad, J. (1975). *The dynamics of educational change.* New York: McGraw-Hill.

Goodlad, J. (1988, December). Informal remarks made at University of Southern Maine, Portland.

Hall, G., & Loucks, S. (1979). Teacher concerns as a basis for facilitating and personalizing staff development. In A. Lieberman & L. Miller (Eds.), *Staff development: New demands, new realities, new perspectives* (pp. 36–53). New York: Teachers College Press.

Henry, N. B. (Ed.). (1957). *National Society of Student Education Yearbook on Inservice.* (Vol. 56, part 1). Chicago: University of Chicago Press.

Kerchner, C. T. (1989, March). *On not acting like a professor: Notes on encouraging teacher researchers.* Paper presented at the meeting of the American Educational Research Association, San Francisco.

Lambert, L. (1988). Staff development redesigned. *Phi Delta Kappan, 69*(9), 665–668.

Lieberman, A., & Miller, L. (Eds.). (1979). *Staff development: New demands, new realities, new perspectives.* New York: Teachers College Press.

Lieberman, A., & Miller, L. (1984). *Teachers, their world and their work: Implications for school improvement.* Alexandria, VA: Association for Supervision and Curriculum Development.

Little, J. W. (1981). *School success and staff development in urban desegregated schools.* Boulder, CO: Center for Action Research.

Little, J. W. (1986). Seductive images and organizational realities in professional development. In A. Lieberman (Ed.), *Rethinking school improvement: Research, craft, and practice* (pp. 26–34). New York: Teachers College Press.

McLaughlin, M., & Marsh, D. (1979). Staff development and school change. In A. Lieberman & L. Miller (Eds.), *Staff development: New demands, new realities, new perspectives* (pp. 69–84). New York: Teachers College Press.

Miller, L. (in press). Curriculum work as staff development. In W. Pink & A. Hyde (Eds.), *Staff development for a change.* Norwood, NJ: Ablex.

Myers, M. (1989, March). *Teacher research: A policy perspective.* Paper presented at the meeting of the American Educational Research Association, San Francisco.

Parker, L. A. (1979). *Networks for innovation and problem solving and their use for improving education: A comparative view.* Washington, DC: Dissemination Processes Seminar, IV.

Rosenholtz, S. (1989). *Teachers' workplace.* New York: Longman.

Sarason, S. (1982). *The culture of the school and the problem of change.* Newton, MA: Allyn & Bacon.

Schaefer, R. J. (1967). *The school as a center of inquiry.* New York: Harper & Row.

Schön, D. (1983). *The reflective practitioner.* San Francisco: Jossey-Bass.

Schön, D. (1987). *Educating the reflective practitioner.* San Francisco: Jossey-Bass.

Sergiovanni, T. (1987). The theoretical basis for cultural leadership. In L. Sheive & M. Schoenhert (Eds.), *Leadership: Examining the elusive* (pp. 116–130). Alexandria, VA: Association for Supervision and Curriculum Development.

Sizer, T. R. (1984). *Horace's compromise: The dilemma of the American high school.* Boston: Houghton Mifflin.

Soo Hoo, S. (1989, March). *Teacher researcher: Emerging change agent.* Paper presented at the meeting of the American Educational Research Association, San Francisco.

Wasley, P. (1989). *The reform rhetoric and the real practice: A study of lead teachers*. Unpublished doctoral dissertation, University of Washington.

Wigginton, E. (1989). Foxfire grows up. *Harvard Educational Review, 59*(1), 24–49.

# 6 | Institutional Standard-Setting in Professional Practice Schools: Initial Considerations

## HOLLY M. HOUSTON

The purpose of a professional practice school is different from that of a conventional school or teacher training program. The mission of such a school might read as follows:

> Student success will be the goal around which the professional practice school is organized. Within this context, the education and socialization of novice teachers is to be a central responsibility of the faculty. The work of teachers, administrators, and clinical faculty will be judged in terms of its relationship to student success. Manifestations of institutional purpose should be found in the school's research priorities, professional development activities, and the daily discourse and actions of adults and students.

With such a mission, the process of designing a professional practice school cannot be approached as the simple grafting of teacher education onto existing schools. A professional practice school, I assert, can and should be greater than the sum of its parts.

The following discussion invites our consideration of an intellectual building code for professional practice schools. This code does not specify standards or the means for measuring compliance with it, but it does outline the sine qua non characteristics of a professional practice school. Most important, it points toward an organized vision for programs of professional practice that are outcome-oriented for both youngsters and adults. Unlike many educational programs whose accountability is dependent on "inputs," these new settings will require focused attention on the results of efforts by students, teachers, clinical faculty, and administrators. The professional practice school envisioned here will draw perhaps more than anything else upon our imaginative resources, for it explicitly challenges the conventions of schooling as we know them.

The term *school* will be used to describe the organizational structure

124

for this project, though it is assumed that many institutional interests will be served by a single collaborative venture—namely, a program of professional practice. As in hospital residency programs, it is possible for an institution to wholly or partially devote its resources to providing clinical training for professionals while also serving the needs of clients. This underscores the point that institutional scope and degree of involvement in clinical training will vary by school and is not assumed to be uniform across professional practice sites. Instead, the carefully forged terms of the relationship among sponsoring institutions will be the hallmark of professional practice school programs.

## A BUILDING CODE FOR PROFESSIONAL PRACTICE SCHOOL PROGRAMS

Given that numerous professional practice programs are currently being designed, what should the building code specify as minimal requirements to ensure that these programs are sound?

### Quality of Student Performance

The primary source of information to be used in answering the above question should be the school's students. Do the students display those qualities that the school is designed to elicit? Do they reveal through their conversation, their degree of sportsmanship, their table manners, their questions, their familiarity with resources, their comfort with adults, their tolerance, their craftsmanship, or their products and performances that they have internalized the best that the school has to offer? This is very different from looking at teachers' intentions—in the form of official curricula, texts, and lesson plans—for information about how well the school is doing with respect to its goals.

Saying that we should look to the students for vital information about the school assumes that the students are routinely called on to perform or to apply their knowledge. Lamentably, most schools today are not built around such expectations for performance or application. Instead they are founded on the assumption that students are to be the passive recipients of someone else's knowledge. The consequence of this is that the majority of students are not taught to *use* their knowledge or skill. Therefore, to make it possible for continuous teacher education to take place around the demonstrated capacities of students, we would want the elicitation of competence to be an organizing characteristic of the school. Toward that end, we would want to ensure that

Students are provided opportunities to demonstrate their knowledge and skill in ways that are responsibly diverse and equitable, thus providing teachers, parents, policy makers, and students themselves with multiple and authentic indices of learning.

Beyond recognizing this as a fundamental aspect of the building code, what other indicators might confirm that we are building a sound structure? One place to look is at a range of tests, exams, contests, performances, quizzes, exhibits, and displays. We could collect these visual, written, and recorded artifacts and analyze them as data—looking not just at how students do but also at how well teachers do as constructors of challenges. The collection would itself tell a story about what the school believes to be important. In effect, the *de facto* values of the school would be revealed, and they might or might not accord with the professed values.

We might also look to the promotion and graduation requirements for evidence that students are being asked to demonstrate knowledge and skill. Do youngsters have to pass over appropriate hurdles in order to move to the next level of work? Do the students believe the hurdles to be worthwhile? Is there a public dimension to their hurdling? What does graduation signify?

Related to these sources of evidence but deserving further elaboration is the role that self-assessment could play in the evaluation of products and performances. We might systematically collect students' and teachers' self-assessments in order to get some measure of the degree of internalization of standards and expectations.

## Teachers' Orientation to Educational Problem Solving

If we wanted to get a feel for the depth of teachers' commitment to this performance-oriented approach to teaching and learning, we might then inquire about the degree to which reflection upon practice and refinement of the assessment tools takes place. We must again decide how to ask for such information and where to look for evidence to support the answers we are given. One line of questioning might evolve from our concern about whether adults are inclined routinely to investigate the effects of their teaching on students' learning. (If they are so inclined, the evidence will reveal that they understand teaching to be an inherently problematic endeavor, rather than a highly routinized activity.) Are there signs that the faculty routinely is in the process of inventing practice around clear expectations for adult and student performance? Very simply, we should find that

There is evidence of an orientation to educational problem solving and re-search that is experimental and collaborative in nature.

If we were to inspect a well-built professional practice school, we would find that research and experimentation *have resulted in* practices that truly enhance student learning and the life of the organization. Examples of research results that would be beneficial in this way might include the following:

- Changes in teaching practice and curriculum content that promote depth of understanding as opposed to mere coverage
- Patterns of classroom interaction that encourage students to be the active initiators of their own learning
- Structures for human interaction that promote trust and accept-ance of responsibility
- The adoption of daily rituals and procedures that promote a feel-ing of community
- Achievement of greater respect on the part of state and district au-thorities for the needs and capabilities of educators
- More effective strategies for inducting new teachers into the pro-fession
- An array of practices that better systematize teaching, learning, and organizational life

We should also find evidence that inquiry along these lines is valued. Such evidence may appear in the form of specific incentives or enabling mechanisms at both the school and district levels that contribute to a person's ability and inclination to engage in work of this kind. This work should be important enough to warrant the systematic compilation of those problems and issues that individuals and teams have addressed through experimentation. From this, feedback loops of program evalua-tion should evolve that yield information about practices that tangibly improve instruction and learning.

## Emphasis on Experimentation and Reflection for Novice Teachers

Another characteristic of any profession whose practices have been fully institutionalized is organized and collective concern about the entry of novices into the field. Just as we would seek some indication that the intellectual life of the school is vigorous by virtue of adults' participation in continuous inquiry into their practice, we should expect also to see concern over the grooming of the next generation of teachers and administrators. More directly, we should find that

> The induction of novice teachers into the teaching profession is structured to provide maximum opportunity for responsible experimentation and reflection on teaching and learning.

This suggests that teaching is not merely a craft to be learned through apprenticeship to a master craftsperson. Rather, teaching simultaneously is an art, a science, and "a calling" whose mysteries each person must enter by himself or herself. In place of the ubiquitous "methods" courses that often do little more than arm the neophyte with defensive strategies to employ when things go in an unexpected (or unhoped-for) direction, we would hope to find novice teachers engaged in careful looking, listening, and collaboration with their more experienced peers. In short, we would expect to see novices learning to inquire about teaching and learning in a disciplined and rigorous manner.

We should also expect to find carefully staged phases of entry into teaching. These stages would reflect the understanding that one's collegiate and graduate preparation are merely starting points in a developmental process that takes years to fully ripen and bear fruit. The stages might also reflect the belief that such learning can be hastened by means of deft collaborative efforts among adults in schools.

## Understanding of Individual Responsibilities

Finally, to emphasize the important role that each adult—novice and veteran—plays in a school organized around clear purposes (or outcomes), we should inquire about how each person defines his or her responsibilities. We would want to find that

> Educators understand the mission of the institution and their individual roles and responsibilities.

Inspection of a professional practice school should yield up-to-date descriptions of each person's responsibilities. We should also find that each person is able to talk in an insightful manner about his or her own role in relationship to student learning, professional collaboration, and the larger mission of the institution. Embedded in these job descriptions should be incentives for teachers and administrators to work in responsible and experimental ways toward the improvement of practice.

And, if performance appraisal serves the purpose of helping to align practice with professed values, we should expect that there will be a need for personnel evaluation in these educational settings. But rather than seeing checklists designed to satisfy the need for efficiency and accountability, we should expect to see evaluations based on the results of carefully documented research projects conducted by teachers to study the effects of their teaching on student learning. The salient questions to be answered by these evaluations should include the following:

- Have teachers deeply internalized their responsibility for evoking learning in students?
- Are teachers in the business of improving their own practice based on what is learned from their students' performance?
- Have teachers satisfactorily set and met goals for student achievement?

Thus we have four elements of a building code for professional practice school programs.

1. Students are provided opportunities to demonstrate their knowledge and skill in ways that are responsibly diverse and equitable, thus providing teachers, parents, policy makers, and students themselves with multiple and authentic indices of learning.
2. There is evidence of an orientation to educational problem solving and research that is experimental and collaborative in nature.
3. The induction of novice teachers into the teaching profession is structured to provide maximum opportunity for responsible experimentation and reflection on teaching and learning.
4. Educators understand the mission of the institution and their individual roles and responsibilities.

## ONE IMPLICATION OF THIS FRAMEWORK FOR PROFESSIONAL PRACTICE

If we assume that professional practice school programs will emerge as the joint responsibility of schools (or school districts) and collegiate teacher education programs, then we should also assume that their success will depend on the coherence of this articulation. It will be important to promote extensive discussion about the institutional traits discussed here and their intersection with the qualities and characteristics of schools and colleges that are scrutinized by established accreditation mechanisms. Because standards for accreditation of schools and colleges and credentialing procedures for public school teachers will invariably affect professional practice schools in the future, it is important to consider a vehicle for standard setting that will ensure an alignment of accreditation and credentialing practices. An analogous situation is found in the field of medicine, as depicted in Table 6.1.

Notable is the absence of an equivalent to medicine's accreditation of postgraduate medical residency programs in hospitals. (In medicine, the formal mechanisms for this program accreditation are the Residency Review Committees of the Accreditation Council for Graduate Medical Education.)

Looking more closely at the rationale for accrediting medical residency programs, we learn that the intersection of credentialing and accreditation is quite pronounced during this phase of medical training and education. It is during this phase of professional activity that residents complete the training requirements of their chosen speciality board (whose exams they must pass for board certification). Each specialty board "generally requires that graduate medical education be obtained in a program reviewed and approved by the Residency Review Committee for that speciality" (American Medical Association, 1985, p. 8). The "general requirements" for the accreditation of residency programs are introduced as follows:

> Programs in graduate medical education are sponsored by institutions engaged in providing medical care and health services. The principal institu-

**Table 6.1 Responsibility for accreditation in medicine and education**

| *In medicine there are several intersecting accrediting agencies whose subjects include:* | *The equivalent responsibilities in the field of education are managed by:* |
|---|---|
| Individual practitioners within various areas of medical speciality | Teacher licensing and certification agencies at the state or national level (e.g., Teacher Credentialing; National Board for Professional Teaching Standards) |
| Four-year medical education programs in colleges and universities | Agencies that accredit postsecondary education programs of teacher education (e.g., American Association of Colleges for Teacher Education; National Council for the Accreditation of Teacher Education) |
| Postgraduate medical residency programs in hospitals | |
| The settings where care is provided (e.g., hospitals) | The regional school accreditation organizations (e.g., the Middle States Association of Colleges and Schools) |

tions for graduate medical education are hospitals. . . . Providing education, training and health services of the highest quality must be a major mission. Graduate medical education requires that residents be directly involved in providing patient care under supervision in an institution that accepts responsibility for the quality of its educational programs. The educational mission must not be compromised by an excessive reliance on residents to fulfill institutional service obligations. Excellence in patient care must not be compromised or jeopardized by needs and prerogatives of educational programs or of research. (p. 9)

We can assume that education's equivalent to these "general requirements" (and the concomitant "standards of practice" that would emerge from these requirements) will be hammered out by appropriately self-interested professional organizations whose collective aim will be to ensure high quality programs of education and service provision. But if this example from medicine proves to be an even modestly predictive analog to conditions we will face in education, then we will need to think carefully about the intersection of professional practice program accreditation and individual teacher certification. If the expectations and requirements for one are not interwoven with those for the other, we will see repeated compromises in standards of quality.

## CONCLUSION

This discussion has focused on a few carefully selected principles for making exemplary practice a staple of institutional life in schools. The professional practice school's purposes, after all, are to (1) promote student success, (2) induct novice teachers into the profession, and (3) support disciplined inquiry directed at the improvement of practice. Such a school is not meant to offer merely an alternative approach to student teaching. (One could argue that to rearrange student teaching practice without first undertaking internal improvements directed at enhancing student and teacher performance would be misguided and, in some cases, irresponsible.) It is assumed that the core values that have been proposed in the form of a building code for professional practice schools would be as useful during the early phases of planning as in framing criteria for *post hoc* judging of institutional success.

For these values to be truly beneficial to persons who have set out to create alternative structures for schooling, however, they would need to be subjected to careful negotiation. Persons who are inventing the professional practice school will need to argue about their expectations and dicker over where to look for evidence that a common vision is being honored. And in recognition of the fact that the creation of these institutions will take time, the designers will need to identify "progress points" in order to track their incremental steps toward loftier goals.

The intersecting institutional responsibilities that this work suggests will require careful negotiation among policy makers as well. And while the point has been made that an external accreditation process will certainly prove beneficial to those involved in professional practice programs, it should be understood that such a process by itself will be an inadequate device for ensuring quality. Hand-in-hand with program accreditation must go a reappraisal of the purposes and expected outcomes of schooling, as well as deep self-scrutiny by institutions of higher education as to their responsibilities for practicing what is being preached about the value of teachers.

## REFERENCE

American Medical Association. (1985). *1985–1986 directory of residency training programs* (pp. 7–13). Chicago: Author.

# 7 | Professional Practice Schools in Context: New Mixtures of Institutional Authority

## BARBARA NEUFELD

In a series of recent papers (earlier versions of the chapters in this volume), the AFT Task Force on Professional Practice Schools proposed the creation of schools "designed to be the institutional base for teaching as a profession." Levine and Gendler (1988) explain that such organizations, known as professional practice schools, would be

> local public elementary or secondary schools specially designed by a collaborative of university, school district, and teachers' unions. Their purpose [would be] threefold: to support student success; to provide a professional induction program for new teachers; and to support systematic inquiry directed toward the improvement of practice. (p. 27)

Those who worked in them would construe teaching as neither standardized nor prescriptive, stressing instead the reflective, inquiring, situational, and analytical aspects of professional practice. This orientation, inventors of the professional practice school concept argue, would lead to teaching that is more tailored to students' needs and thus more likely to lead to student success.

Professional practice schools would be organizations attentive to teacher as well as student learning because the two are integrally related. They would include well-designed, teacher-influenced clinical education programs for preservice and induction-year teachers as well as opportunities for ongoing professional development. In this regard, professional practice schools imply an equal partnership of elementary and secondary school teachers with college faculty in the preparation of new teachers.

By proposing that schools be centers of inquiry, the professional practice school concept places considerable emphasis on the importance of developing usable knowledge about teaching at the school and classroom level. It envisions an institution in which school- and campus-based educators will work toward articulating and utilizing knowledge about teaching and learning generated by *teachers* as well as by campus-based researchers in the preparation of new teachers and in the ongoing work of experienced teachers (Levine & Gendler, 1988). Professionalization of teaching would evolve as a result of teachers' greater responsibility for (1) the preparation of others entering the profession; (2) the production of knowledge about teaching and learning; and (3) the development of standards of adequate teaching performance. Professional practice schools imply a teaching profession with greater responsibility for preparing and monitoring the performance of its members. According to Levine & Gendler (1988), professional practice schools will "address the two issues at the top of the public education agenda today—the problem of how to restructure schools to support student learning and the problems of professionalizing teaching" (p. 27).

There are other proposals for restructuring schools, creating new kinds of relations with teacher preparation institutions, professionalizing teaching, and, of course, improving student learning.[1] The concept of professional practice schools, however, represents the emergence of teachers' voices in the conversation about school reform. They join schools of education, state departments of education, and local districts, all of which have been wrestling with what to do to improve teaching and learning and all of which have a great stake in the future of schools and of teaching. And they join the conversation in an environment already rich with programs and proposals striving to alter traditional ways of teaching children and preparing teachers.

Professional practice schools have been proposed in a context that has only recently become attentive, however, to the role of the school as the locus for improving teaching and learning, and to teachers as a prime source of professional knowledge. That new attention is growing in the midst of deeply rooted teacher education traditions that construe the university as the source of knowledge about teaching. Even though teachers (and often teacher educators) acknowledge the shortcomings of traditional teacher education, as yet they have little experience with alternatives. Finally, professional practice schools have been proposed in the context of a slew of newly implemented state education policies, many of which reflect a bureaucratic, hierarchical orientation to reform that emphasizes the external, centralized prescription and monitoring of teachers' work. Such an approach is different from the emphasis on local program development and practitioner-generated knowledge intrinsic to professional practice schools.

This being the environment, what would be involved in designing and implementing the AFT's vision of professional practice schools? As teachers and teacher education programs try to create such schools, what will be likely points of conflict and compatibility between them and the contexts in which they operate? What kind of formal and informal stumbling blocks and constraints might such efforts face? What traditions and standard operating procedures would be challenged? What kinds of extant policies would militate against the creation of such institutions? What features of the policy and practice environments would support and facilitate design and implementation? For no matter how good the concept of professional practice schools may be in theory, it is doubtful that it can be nurtured, and thereby tested in practice, in every locale. Some settings, because of distant and recent approaches to school and teacher education reform, will be more hospitable. Others will be less so. If we wish to attempt professional practice schools, it makes sense to seek nourishing contexts for their inception and development. What might those contextual features be that work for and against professional practice schools?

This chapter begins an exploration of these questions by playing out the idea of professional practice schools in light of some of the contexts in which they would be created. It looks specifically at what is implied for teacher education institutions and for schools, and the likely interaction of organizational and professional requirements of professional practice schools with extant and forthcoming state policies designed to improve teaching and learning, as well as the status of teachers. For the discussion of school/university collaborations, I draw primarily on the combined experiences of several recent collaborations in Massachusetts (Neufeld & Haavind, 1988), New York (interviews with teacher educators and school district and state personnel knowledgeable about the collaborative venture in Rochester), and Connecticut (Neufeld, 1989). For the connections between professional practice schools and state policy, I will present examples of several states' reforms and the likely impact of both the policy strategy they employ and the content of their policies on professional practice schools. Massachusetts, New York, Connecticut, and Florida present fruitful examples with which to play out the interaction of professional practice schools with a variety of approaches to policy. These states' policies vary in the extent to which they

- Employ mandates or encourage voluntary participation
- Specify the organization and content of teacher education at the preservice and induction levels or enable teachers and college faculty to design programs at the local level

- Emphasize teachers as individuals or schools as work organizations in their reform strategies

As such, these approaches to policy structure and content provide contrasting examples with which to play out the implications of developing professional practice schools. Exploring the implications will enable those interested in pursuing the possibilities of creating professional practice schools to extrapolate to a variety of state policies and contexts.

## SCHOOL/UNIVERSITY COLLABORATIONS

Traditionally, school/college collaborations are formed with the goal of improving the field-based component of preservice teacher education by involving classroom teachers more closely with the program offered on campus. Collaborations provide stability in locating and refining field placements. Teacher educators aim to increase the skill and frequency with which classroom teachers provide learning opportunities to student teachers that are congruent with the programs' goals. Often, these learning opportunities are represented by a set of activities and experiences— development of a curriculum unit, experience with whole-class and group instruction, and attendance at parent conferences, for example. Colleges might prefer to work with classroom teachers who have particular teaching styles, but teaching style has been less important than the teacher's willingness to allow the student to practice teach.

Collaborations, then, often are formally shaped by the knowledge, skill, and goals defined by the college: The teacher education program helps teachers understand what it wants students to experience during student teaching and other field experiences. Only rarely do programs involve teachers as informants to the college on the shape and content of the field experience or accompanying seminars and methods courses. The college also determines the standards by which prospective teachers' teaching will be judged, and retains the authority to judge teaching quality even though the student's practice has occurred under the tutelage of the cooperating teacher. Traditional collaborations require little or no reform on the part of the larger organizations in which they exist because roles and authority relations remain fundamentally unchanged. They maintain the view of teaching as a craft learned, in large part, through apprenticeship with an experienced mentor.

Professional practice schools, in contrast, would require changes in roles, role relations, ideas about teaching practice and teacher education, and the allocation of authority. As the AFT's *Radius* (Levine, 1988) puts it,

> Teachers as a faculty, and in collaboration with administrators and university faculty, will have to agree upon standards of practice. They will have to collaboratively evaluate and review practice in their schools; focus on the individual and collective needs of students; work together with university faculty in teaching and conducting research, and supervising interns. (p.3)

Professional practice schools will pose new challenges because they require us to alter our image of teachers from one of *lone practitioners* working with groups of students to one of *members of collegial teaching teams* that support inquiry into practice as a professional norm. Prospective and induction-year teachers will need field experiences that reinforce these new notions of the nature of professional practice (see Kennedy, 1988, and Chapter 3 of this volume for details). In order for them to have such experiences, the culture of schools—the standard ways of doing things—will have to undergo major changes. The professional practice school will be a new institution.

What does this new institution with new roles and responsibilities imply for school/university collaborations in teacher preparation and induction? Which issues will be similar and which different from those found in traditional arrangements? What should potential developers of such schools keep in mind as they begin the process? Because such schools do not exist, the best we can do is imagine how the *set of ideas and proposed practices* differs from what is traditional, and play out the implications as they might develop for teacher preparation programs, classroom teachers, schools, and school districts.

## INTER-INSTITUTIONAL ISSUES OF AUTHORITY

Involving classroom teachers and whole schools more seriously in teacher education implies increased authority and influence for the school site. It recognizes that classroom teachers have knowledge and skill to contribute to teacher education programs, and to teacher education outside formal programs, and that their role is not merely to better translate the university's program into school practices. This is easy to describe, but those developing professional practice schools will have to grapple with a bundle of thorny issues that logically follow. What kind of influence should teachers have and who should decide? Might they have a formal role in evaluating future teachers; in making decisions about the content of both the field experience and the on-campus components of teacher education programs? How might teachers' perspectives change what and how college faculty teach? How will disagreements be resolved? Who will decide whether classroom teachers' participation in college courses is advantageous in general; whether a particular teacher or faculty member is sufficiently knowledgeable and skillful? Who, in the professional practice school, will be in charge of teacher education and responsible for its outcomes?

Issues of authority are certainly about control of knowledge, but they are also about fundamental resources: job descriptions and job security. New ideas about more equal collaborations may pose immediate threats to faculty in teacher education institutions because they propose increased roles for classroom teachers. Faculty may see the shift in authority suggested by professional practice schools as a zero sum game in which they lose. Activities in two recently formed collaborations provide examples related to these issues.

The first concerns a university's effort to revise its core teacher education program. The university is involved with a local school system in a collaborative enterprise that has as its goal some restructuring of schools and the creation of clinical training sites. Nonetheless, the revision of the teacher education program has been planned entirely by university faculty. The program director hopes teachers in the school district will like and support the revisions. If not, the university will listen to their suggestions and make changes. This is a familiar model of program development, one that asks for teacher input *after* the development phase of a project. In a professional practice school collaboration, one might expect teacher involvement at the program design/development stage, in which classroom teachers' experience with student teachers would be informative. Such involvement, however, requires a major shift in thinking about roles, expertise, and authority on the part of both college faculty and schoolteachers.

A second example of an authority issue concerns the question of who will formally evaluate student teachers when teachers have a greater role in the clinical aspects of teacher education. Traditionally, the college has been responsible for assigning grades even though the cooperating teacher spends more time with the student teacher. In a professional practice school in which teachers have a greater role in teacher education and the development of standards of professional practice, one can imagine teachers expecting to have the authority to apply those standards to prospective teachers. Colleges may not be eager to share that authority with classroom teachers. Although they may support the notion of a professional practice school, they may feel that they are losing an important source of authority and control of teacher education.

Even when faculty are willing to share the authority to assign grades to classroom teachers, university rules and regulations may require changes to make it possible. At one ongoing collaboration designed to lead to a restructured school, long-standing university rules passed by the board of trustees require faculty to assign grades for all university work. Unless the rules are changed, cooperating teachers cannot assign "official" grades to student teachers. In this instance, even though the professor assigns the official grade, the cooperating teacher's opinion of student teachers is included via a letter of recommendation in the student's file. Additional evaluation/authority issues will arise as the apprenticeship model of one student teacher working with one cooperating teacher is replaced by arrangements in which students work with an array of teachers. Not only will the role of the college have to be renegotiated, but classroom teachers will have to work together to come to some agreements about the quality of student teachers' work. This is a desired outcome, but one that will require considerable time and thought to implement.

## SCHOOL DISTRICT ISSUES RELATED TO COLLABORATION

Most often, professional practice schools will begin in school districts that operate under the traditional system of school organization and governance. As a result, in the short run at least, professional practice schools with their restructured organization and emphasis on inquiry and teacher education will be unconventional in their settings. Districts will be in the position of nurturing a new organization, whose successes might be the source of future innovation, while simultaneously sustaining the old order. To pursue the traditional and the new, school district administrators and school committees/boards will have made some initial decisions about (1) hopes and goals for a professional practice school, (2) design considerations, (3) implementation issues, and ultimately, (4) evaluation of the school as a whole and its various components. These decisions will be important because they will provide both a rationale and a process by which districts deal with the following kinds of potential complications.

### Educational Concerns

Central office personnel will be faced with explaining the connection between district goals and objectives and the educational activities in professional practice schools. For example, an urban district that is encouraging a professional practice school may have established a policy for improving student achievement by requiring specific test scores prior to promotion. The professional practice school faculty may wish to improve student achievement not through setting cutoff scores but through an organization that looks at students' progress over two years instead of one and that uses multiple measures of achievement in determining promotion. Even if the school district allows the professional practice school to pursue its different approach, one can imagine problems arising for the district and for the individual schools. Children in one school will be retained while others with similar, even identical, characteristics will not. Questions of fairness will be raised, as will questions about whether the district knows what will be effective. Some may claim that the district is "experimenting" with or "punishing" the community's children.

Or, imagine that a district adopts an inservice teaching improvement model such as the one offered by Madeline Hunter. Teachers in professional practice schools may have to obtain waivers to exempt themselves from the requirement to use the adopted instructional strategy (and from the associated evaluation schemes that often are tied to such programs). To do otherwise would contradict the definition of professional practice underlying the professional practice school. The issue highlights what is frequently a tension between the push toward standardization and control and that toward development of teachers' professional judgment in matters of teaching and learning. The district granting a waiver would find itself in the position of having to justify two competing theories of school and teaching improvement.

Ideally, in these and other situations, the professional practice school and, perhaps, the research and evaluation offices of the district will find themselves designing research/evaluation studies to determine the relative efficacy of their approaches to issues of teaching and learning. The development of such inquiry as an ongoing part of school policy making is one potential benefit of the professional practice schools' presence in the district. It suggests, however, district commitment to change that extends beyond the walls of the professional practice school to the district as a whole. (For further discussion, see Levine, 1988.)

Thinking more broadly, districts will want to ensure that schools set realistic goals for their teacher education and professional development work. Although a primary purpose of professional practice schools is to improve student learning, it is likely that districts will remain concerned that programs not become overly ambitious or too heavily involved in teacher education, thus drawing attention away from their central task of teaching children. Districts will have to be particularly attentive to parents' concerns. On the one hand, parents may worry about the extent to which their children will be taught by novices and/or student teachers. On the other hand, parents whose children are not in professional practice schools may feel that their children are being denied the enriched programs that result from such schools' attention to teaching, curriculum, and research. Equity and quality are likely to become concerns as these reforms move forward.

## Staffing/Contract Considerations

Involvement in collaborative teacher education ventures and efforts to broaden teachers' roles will likely require contract negotiations that relate, for example, to teachers' job descriptions, transfer rights, release time, salary, and scheduling changes. Districts will assuredly be involved in staffing considerations. If the professional practice school is seen as something in which teachers across the district want to share, the contract may have to deal with transfers into and out of those schools. These kinds of staffing decisions may become issues for collective bargaining, regardless of whether teachers receive additional or differential compensation for their work in professional practice schools.

There will also be job description and authority issues that directly affect principals of professional practice schools and indirectly affect those who remain in the district's traditional schools. At the simplest level, it is not clear what role principals will fulfill in a school in which teachers are responsible for decisions about teaching and learning and acceptable standards of practice. Not too long ago, principals' stars had risen; they were identified as key to school improvement efforts through their role as instructional leaders (Manasse, 1982). Teachers have eclipsed them in this latest reform wave, even though formally principals remain responsible for teaching and learning in their schools. Experiences with pilot professional development school programs in Massachusetts and an early version of the mentor program in Connecticut suggest that, in most cases, the principal's role in restructured schools or in schools that remain traditional in organization but provide new roles for teachers is not part of ongoing discussions. Principals who had marginal status in several of these pilot programs noted that they would like

- A role in deciding whether such programs are established in their schools in the first place
- A role in making staffing decisions for such programs
- Assistance or a shift in responsibility so that they can oversee the implementation of school/college collaborations
- District support to facilitate implementation (Neufeld, 1986, Neufeld & Haavind, 1988)

These desires are reasonable, but they understate the depth and significance of changes in school-site organization and governance that are likely to accompany the creation of professional practice schools. At the very least, (1) teachers will have a broader array of roles, (2) some budgetary discretion will be granted to the professional practice school (even if full-fledged school-based management is not implemented), and (3) university/school collaborations will create inter-institutional relationships that have implications for management. As professional practice schools take form, it is certain that the nature of administrative work in schools will change. As Sykes and Elmore (1989) suggest, this would be a good thing, given the impossible demands on administrators in the current organization.

> Fitting people into impossible roles and structures, relying on their coping behavior, and lionizing their successes does not constitute an effective, long-term strategy for the improvement of schooling. Instead we must create conditions for the invention of new structures that enable the emergence of leadership on a broad basis. (pp. 78–79)

Professional practice schools can "create conditions for the invention" of such structures. As with the creation of such conditions and structures for teachers, this will occur at the local level, within the context of the school and the district. Thus, the role and responsibility of principals is an issue with which the district as well as the professional practice school will have to wrestle.

## Fiscal Considerations

Fiscal issues will accompany the new, nonteaching roles for teachers, school/university staffing relationships, and (perhaps) external funding. Nonteaching (but nonadministrative) roles such as mentor, student teaching supervisor, school-based leader of the student teaching seminar, curriculum developer, and teacher-researcher will remove teachers from classrooms so they can engage in a broad array of professional responsibilities that are not directly instructional but are designed to serve the needs of students and intern teachers. Districts will have to replace such personnel in classrooms. Alternative funding (perhaps from the district, perhaps not) will be required to support the new positions. In their collaborative role with the campus-based teacher education program, classroom teachers may teach at the college on their own time and be paid as adjunct faculty by the college, or they may be released from part of their normal teaching load in order to engage in teacher education work. In the first model, an arrangement that is fairly typical without school/university collaborations, there is no financial cost to the district. In the latter model, the district may be involved in arranging the cost of covering the instructional time of released teachers.

Whatever the situation, the district will remain responsible for financial decisions and accounting procedures. Districts will be important not only because their approval for expenditures will influence program implementation, but because they will have to manage the potentially complicated professional practice school accounts. For example, under one foundation-funded collaboration, expert practitioners from the district's secondary schools cotaught a year-long seminar with university faculty members. The teacher and professor formed a team that worked with student teacher placements as well as with the ongoing seminar. The financial arrangement involved the university's using foundation money to pay the district's portion of the teachers' salaries to make this release time from high school teaching possible. In other words, high school teachers were not paid directly by the university, although the university paid for their involvement in the collaboration. The district had additional financial management tasks associated with this arrangement.

### Evaluation

School districts will no doubt want to evaluate professional practice schools to determine whether they are educationally advantageous and cost effective. In deciding to support the development of a professional practice school, districts will likely have articulated goals for the enterprise, which, if achieved, would make it worthwhile. Administrators, teachers, and perhaps parents will have expressed ideas about how and why such a school would benefit the district. Locally directed inquiry may be needed to determine the extent to which the professional practice school is achieving its and the district's goals. Districts will need to take responsibility for generating this kind of information as they remain accountable to their publics. Such research-based information would also be useful in a formative sense to determine the next steps in the development of the school and to define the insights, activities, arrangements, and strategies that might transfer to other schools in the district.

## COLLEGE FACULTY ISSUES RELATED TO COLLABORATION

Professional practice schools would likely lead to alterations in college faculty work. It is not clear whether faculty would be more heavily invested in the school site or whether they would turn over more of the clinical work to public school teachers, but either change would have consequences from the perspective of some faculty members. Given the promotion structure of most colleges, which reward faculty for research and publishing but not for support of clinical work, if faculty spend more time in field settings, they may jeopardize promotion and tenure decisions. One faculty member noted ironically that it was easier to be promoted "by holing up in your office to write about teachers and collaboration than by actually getting involved in the schools." Some colleges report initiatives to reward faculty work in schools with salary increments, a practice that would facilitate school/college collaborations, but promotion and tenure decisions still rest heavily on publishing. If colleges encourage participation in professional practice schools, they may need to restructure their incentive system so that participating faculty are not penalized. It is not at all clear that colleges would be interested in such a shift. If they are not, then their most likely organizational response would be to staff programs with adjunct or clinical professors who hold second-class status in the university.

Job security presents another, equally troublesome issue likely to be associated with involving classroom teachers more formally in clinical work. For example, one collaborative program proposed having a high school teacher serve as the college's supervisor for a student teacher in an effort to develop a clinical appointment for the high school teacher. College faculty members objected to this transfer of authority and to what they saw as a threat to their jobs. The proposal was not implemented. Those involved in creating professional practice schools will have to devise creative staffing solutions in light of these legitimate concerns.

One additional issue for colleges concerns the involvement of liberal arts faculty in teacher education. As programs ask students to spend greater amounts of time in the liberal arts (an emphasis that seems to be growing across the country at both the elementary and secondary levels), they will spend less time with teacher education faculty. But if programs take seriously both content and pedagogy, then liberal arts faculty may be called on to visit schools in order to consult on and assess subject-matter pedagogy. This will create the same tenure/promotion issues raised earlier with respect to teacher education faculty. Liberal arts faculty assuredly have little institutional support for spending time in schools. They may have little personal interest in doing so, complicating the process of creating new roles and responsibilities.[2]

Joint appointments will be similarly problematic. For example, one teacher education program is considering hiring a subject-matter specialist jointly with the science department at the collaborating university. If such a person was hired, he or she would have to play according to the rules for tenure and promotion set by the science department. This would militate against involvement in a site-based approach to teacher education that would require time in schools for which the science department offered no rewards.

## IDEAS ABOUT LEARNING TO TEACH

No one seriously disputes the importance of classroom teaching experience for prospective teachers, and yet the content (in contrast to the structure) of that experience gets surprisingly little explicit attention. Teacher education programs and cooperating teachers might agree that prospective teachers should have experience teaching algebra to two different levels of students, for example, but they rarely discuss what it is that prospective teachers should learn about teaching, or about teaching algebra, or about teaching different kinds of learners, from those experiences. And they rarely discuss what cooperating teachers need to know and be able to do in order to help student teachers achieve those goals.

The thinking that will go into creating professional practice schools is an opportunity to address

1. What prospective teachers should learn from the field-based component of their teacher education programs
2. How the experience might be structured to facilitate that learning
3. What classroom teachers and college faculty need to know and how they might learn it in order to be most helpful to prospective teachers

Several researchers observing the relationship between clinical experience and learning to teach point out the lack of attention to content and the potentially conservative impact of classroom teaching experience on ultimate teaching practice (see, for example, Feiman-Nemser & Buchmann, 1983; Schlechty & Whitford, 1989; Zeichner, 1985). As several of the extant programs demonstrate, collaborative ventures provide a context in which practitioners' wisdom can contribute to the knowledge brought by university faculty. Jointly held seminars that involve school and university faculty in designing and implementing the student teaching seminar and in deciding what should be included in the student teaching experience are efforts to think explicitly and creatively about the content as well as the structure of teaching and other school experiences for prospective and induction-year teachers.

## Ideas About the Nature of Teaching

As collaborations form they will confront their own views about the nature of teaching, learning, and learning to teach, in particular. Much teacher education poses a model of teaching, and learning to teach, as the acquisition of craft knowledge. The assignment of novices to individual experienced teachers reflects this orientation. By emulating the master teacher, the novice has the opportunity to learn the craft. Proposals that call for the assignment of novices to more than one cooperating teacher or mentor do not necessarily change this orientation to teaching as craft. Instead, they point out that any one "master" has a limited array of talents. Increasing the number of masters broadens the novices' craft knowledge.

Professional practice schools aim to create a cadre of teachers who think of teaching as *intellectual work*—work that involves them in transforming knowledge about teaching as well as creating it through inquiry into practice. To do this, professional practice schools propose that teachers and teacher educators become what Schön (1987) calls reflective practitioners. This requirement poses substantial problems for the creation of such schools. The term *reflective practice* is used frequently these days but it is not clear that it is used with meaning beyond the idea that teachers give some thought to their teaching both as they are doing it and after the fact. With respect to learning to teach, it similarly implies opportunities to talk about practice. Such conversations, however, merely by being "about teaching," do not necessarily embody the ideas that Schön proposes and the Task Force embraces. Even if they are structured so that teachers share their ideas, consider alternative strategies, and make joint decisions, such teacher activity will not necessarily result in practice much different from what we currently see as the best of traditional teaching. It may result in improved, but not different, practice, just as infusing classroom teaching with activities does not necessarily alter the conceptions of knowledge provided to children. To develop *different practice*—teaching that encourages children to actively construct their own knowledge, and teacher education that encourages teachers to do the same with respect to learning to teach—teachers have to learn what the idea means for themselves as learners, and they must learn how to work with children in a way that is supportive of such learning.

The first three questions with which professional practice schools must grapple in their formative phase are, therefore,

1. What exactly is this orientation to teaching?
2. What does it imply for learning to teach?
3. How will it play out in real schools?

Without doubt, teaching that encourages children to construct their own knowledge will place enormous, as well as novel, demands on teachers (Cohen, 1988). The next two questions are

4. Who already understands and uses this orientation to teaching and learning to teach?
5. How will schools be organized so that others can learn?

And finally, if no one in the district or teacher education program currently uses this approach (which would not be surprising),

6. What will be the process by which a cadre of teachers and teacher educators learns to work in this way?[3]

A significant hurdle, in other words, is likely to loom large at the outset, because the core construction of teaching practice and learning to teach proposed for professional practice schools is neither common in practice nor even very familiar. In such circumstances, it is likely that the professional practice school created will differ only marginally from what went before with respect to ideas about teaching and learning to teach.

## A Note About Students

Professional practice schools will be designed to support student success, yet this discussion has not mentioned students. It has spoken to several organizational and substantive issues involved in forming collaborations to improve and change the nature of preservice teacher education and the role of teachers in that enterprise. It has focused on teachers and teacher educators and the adult aspects of the organizations in which they work. This focus is not meant to minimize the host of issues that concern students and must be dealt with as professional practice schools are developed. An exploration of those issues is beyond the scope of this chapter, but they must be considered as new organizations and roles are created. No one intends for students to become lost in efforts to make schools "the institutional base for teaching as a profession" (Levine, 1988; also see Pechman, 1990, and Chapter 2 of this volume).

## SUMMARY: SCHOOL/UNIVERSITY COLLABORATIONS

Creating professional practice schools requires a unique kind of collaboration between the organizations most heavily involved in the enterprise—the public schools and the colleges and universities. It is unique because it asks each organization to change, to alter the pattern of authority relations that have characterized past associations, to reorganize work within schools, and to rethink the nature and source of knowledge about teaching and learning to teach that ought to inform the preparation of new teachers. It is also unique because it asks each institution to reconstrue the nature of teaching practice from one of craft to one of intellectual work. Thus, the formation of professional practice schools will not be a straightforward organizational or conceptual task. For the parties involved, it will be an adventure that requires a good bit of risk-taking, a tolerance for not "getting it right" the first time, and a firm commitment to long-term goals. The success of the various endeavors will depend, in part, on the knowledge, skill, and fortitude of local participants. It will also depend on the larger political and governance context in which attempts to form professional practice schools take place. For that reason, the next section of the chapter explores the potential impact of the state policy context on the formation of professional practice schools.

## PROFESSIONAL PRACTICE SCHOOLS IN STATE CONTEXTS

Public schools are governed by locally elected school boards. If such boards decide they would like to create professional practice schools, they have the authority to join into collaborative arrangements with teacher education programs and local teacher unions in order to reorganize schools toward that end. What importance does the state policy context hold, then, for what are fundamentally local decisions? Ten or 15 years ago, state context would likely have had little impact on the organization and implementation of such decisions. The last decade of education reform, however, has changed that. Local efforts today take place in a state policy environment that is complex, comprehensive, and often constraining.

Timar and Kirp (1989) report that in the past 6 years "the states have generated more rules and regulations about all aspects of education than in the previous 20 years" (p. 506). They now attend to issues of curriculum, assessment, teaching methods, homework, course requirements, and eligibility for extracurricular activities, to cite just a few areas addressed by policy. States have increased entry-level teaching salaries, created career ladders, and differentiated staffing plans. They have attempted to improve the quality of beginning teachers by altering course and practicum requirements for the initial, provisional teaching certificate.

Some of this increased oversight and attention, no doubt, is necessary and good. Cuban (1988) and Darling-Hammond (1988) point out that schools, left to their own devices, do not always act in the best interests of all children. They sometimes do what is expedient; they are always subject to competing interests and multiple constituencies, usually in situations of scarce resources and uncertainty about the efficacy of any course of action. Yet, despite the benefits associated with state attention to education, we now know that one unintended outcome of such policy initiatives is an overregulated education system that has a difficult time responding to children's individual needs and in which teachers often work within severe constraints (Darling-Hammond, 1988; Wise, 1979). Policies have reinforced long-standing tendencies for schools to be systems in which, as Darling-Hammond suggests, teachers are rewarded for "doing things right," rather than "doing the right thing."

Current proposals that call for a shift away from rules and regulations toward professionalizing teaching and restructuring school governance aim to restore (or create) professional judgment—doing the right thing—to educational decisions. They aim to ameliorate and, where possible, eliminate rules and regulations that circumscribe teaching practice. Cognizant of the need for higher standards within the teaching force, these proposals call for the creation of stringent entry standards that will be controlled by the profession and not by the state.

But this latest approach to school reform must germinate in the complex state policy environment of heavy intervention and oversight created during the last decade. It must flourish, in other words, in environments that do not appear conducive to growth. Those who wish to create professional practice schools will have to figure out how to work within environments replete with rules and regulations.

Timar and Kirp (1989) point out that the environmental impact of policies, for better or for worse, results not only from their accumulation, but also from the way in which they are construed.

> School reform efforts that ignore the complexities of the policy environment often fail. . . . There is no single policy or single combination of policies—such as merit pay, the use of mentor teachers, teacher competency testing, and stricter teacher certification requirements—that will automatically transform mediocre schools into good ones . . . [but] while specific policies may not be important determinants of school improvement, the strategies that states adopt do make a difference in reform efforts. (p. 506)

The authors sort policy strategies represented by the reform agendas into three basic models.

1. Rational planning, which identifies the problems to be solved and then searches for the correct solutions
2. Market incentives, which rely on state-level policy development and implementation bargained at the local level
3. Political interaction, which stresses the process of decision making and is distinguished by "broad state policy goals, with discretionary authority and flexibility in local implementation. This approach to policy implementation aims to integrate state policy goals with local conditions and practices" (p. 76).

States working within the rational planning model are likely to employ top-down mandates with standardized requirements as their major reform strategy. This approach allows for little local discretion about whether to participate or how to shape the reform to respond to local district conditions. In contrast, the market incentive approach creates artificial markets by making funding available for a set of activities supported by the state. Participation is left to local discretion, as is the opportunity to shape the program to local conditions. Finally, the political interaction model sets out broad state goals toward which districts must work. However, the model encourages districts to become competent in problem solving so that they can develop locally appropriate ways to achieve those goals.

These models describe three dominant policy strategies, but it is important to note that states do not always operate within only one model. In some domains, they may provide incentives; in others, rules and regulations. Even within the same policy domain, states may be inconsistent in their approach to reform. For example, states may applaud in principle the shift to increasing professionalism and school-based decision making, yet their policies may organize district-level accountability in such a way that school-based decision making becomes impossible in many areas. It is fairly common to find, as does Darling-Hammond (1988),

> reform proposals [that] at the same time urge greater involvement of policy makers in shaping schools and greater involvement of teachers in shaping teaching. Consequently, we see states passing laws that pay lip service to teacher professionalism while, with the other hand, they enact greater restraints on curricula, textbooks, tests, and teaching methods. (p. 60)

It is in such contexts that professional practice schools will originate and develop. And, for this reason, it is worthwhile examining the likely interaction of state policy strategies with the ideas that undergird professional practice schools.

## CONTRASTING POLICY STRATEGIES

Anyone who peruses summaries of state legislative action related to education reform quickly learns that the enterprise is neither static nor complete. States continue to adopt new policies and modify older ones. The crises generated by economic downturns can reduce the availability of funds for existing as well as new programs. Any attempt to consider the impact of specific state policies on the development of professional practice schools, then, might seem like a pointless endeavor. The policies discussed, one could argue, might be altered or gone by the time of the reading; or new policies might have changed the context within which older ones exist. To allay such concerns, keep in mind first that as I explore the impact of current policies on the formation and sustenance of professional practice schools, I am concerned with the general strategy of the policy and the area of teacher education that it addresses. I use specific policies only as exemplars.

Second, in selecting specific policies from each state's large array of policies, I am not claiming to represent the complete policy context of each state or suggesting the extent to which the state as a whole would be hospitable to professional practice schools. My goal is to suggest a way to think about the impact of policies in considering the development of professional practice schools. I chose Massachusetts, New York, Florida, and Connecticut because each has one or more policies appropriate to this task. The accumulation of policies in each state will certainly influence the extent to which professional practice schools might flourish, but my purpose in this chapter is *not* a state-by-state consideration.

What is important in judging the likely interaction of state policies with professional practice schools is whether the state policies have an orientation that is compatible or at odds with the underlying philosophy and orientation of professional practice schools. Facilitating policies will

1. Enable schools to develop locally conceived school/college collaborations
2. Support, or at least remain neutral with respect to, new roles for teachers in teacher preparation
3. Sustain or create local authority to develop preparation programs and assessment strategies for those who will work with preservice and novice teachers
4. Support an inquiry approach to teaching as work
5. View teachers as producers as well as consumers of research knowledge
6. Consider the school as the unit of reform

Policies in areas other than these will assuredly influence the organization of teaching and learning and, therefore, professional practice schools. State high school graduation examinations, for example, will influence what is taught and the time by which students must master the material. The implementation of standardized reading and mathematics exams will influence the sequencing and content of some subjects. Policies that circumscribe daily time to be spent on required subject matter or the nature of student evaluation will impede local efforts to create curriculum, organization, and evaluation strategies. These kinds of regulatory and monitoring devices assuredly will interfere with professional practice schools' orientation to teaching, learning, and assessment. Yet one can imagine local adaptations and waivers from at least some of these constraints. The more serious threats to professional practice schools are likely to come from such policies as standardized, behavior-based teacher evaluation or state-defined career ladder plans that construe teaching in terms inappropriate to professional practice schools or preclude the possibility of local program development.

With these kinds of issues in mind, this chapter continues with a discussion of several state policies that relate to three areas pertinent to professional practice schools.

1. Arrangements and requirements for those who support the clinical experience of preservice and first-year teachers
2. Restructuring schools for student and teacher learning
3. The orientation of the state to "good teaching" and to acceptable sources of knowledge about teaching

These are areas that will be critical to the formation of professional practice schools because they are central to the preparation of new teachers and to the role that experienced teachers will have both in their own development and in the preparation of their junior colleagues.

Due to severe negative financial conditions, the future of several of the specific state policies discussed is in doubt. Their demise would certainly change the climate for a host of educational endeavors, including professional practice schools. For the purpose of this discussion, however, the continuation of the policies and programs is not essential. What is instructive for those interested in creating professional practice schools is the policies' orientation to teaching, learning, learning to teach, and school organization. The vulnerability of the current reform agenda to economic conditions is a troubling issue beyond the scope of this chapter.

### The Cooperating Teacher Training Program in Connecticut

The Cooperating Teacher Training Program is one component of Connecticut's comprehensive effort to improve the preparation of beginning teachers and increase the involvement of experienced classroom teachers in that enterprise.[4] The program, aimed at the clinical component of preservice teacher education,

1. Requires prospective teachers who wish Connecticut certification to student teach with "trained" cooperating teachers
2. Outlines the parameters of cooperating teacher training
3. Mandates the organizational structure in which it will take place
4. Provides direct payment to teachers for their work with student teachers
5. Requires teacher participation in decision making relevant to certain aspects of program development and implementation

The program was conceived as one in which campus and field-based teacher educators would merge their strengths to improve student teaching supervision by classroom teachers. The state defined the way in which this merger would occur.

To be specific, Connecticut required the formation of consortia—collaborations of at least two teacher preparation institutions, a regional service center and a set of school districts—to develop training programs that complied with externally developed state guidelines that specified content and duration. These collaborations were, to a great degree, born out of necessity: Colleges were required to work with each other and with school districts in their geographical area if they wanted their graduates to be eligible for state provisional teaching certificates. Thus, if the school/university collaboration that will become the basis of professional practice schools (1) depends on a match between *participants'* purposes and orientation to teaching and learning, and (2) will be developmental with respect to form and content, then state-formed consortia are not likely to serve this function. Based almost exclusively on geography, state-formed consortia were created to accomplish a required, externally defined task. Their existence, however, adds to the complexity of the policy environment in which professional practice school collaborations would be formed.

Connecticut's policy has several other features that complicate movement toward professional practice schools. Their improvement strategy is targeted to individuals, and the incentive structure encourages districts to involve, over time, *all* trained cooperating teachers in order to give them the opportunity to earn the stipend that accompanies the position. This reasonable local accommodation to policy can conflict with a college's desire to cluster its student teachers within particular schools. For the same reason it would likely discourage the development of professional practice schools, wherein teacher education—and so the work of cooperating teachers—would be concentrated.

Two other features of Connecticut's reform policy strategy are worth noting as they bear on the potential development of professional practice schools. By designing a program that sustains the traditional relationship of one cooperating teacher working with one student teacher, the state has adopted a craft model of teaching and learning to teach. While this approach to assisting beginning and preservice teachers may well improve teaching, it is not designed to counter prevailing isolated practice or to create an inquiry approach to teaching and learning to teach. As such, the policy suggests an orientation different from that envisioned for professional practice schools, which would aim to create roles and relationships that stressed collaboration among experienced and novice teachers, and an inquiry, rather than craft, approach to learning to teach.

And last, designation as a "trained" cooperating teacher is based on participation in the program, not on any demonstrable achievement or competence. The absence of standards is an omission that has implications for professional practice schools, in that such schools would likely recognize the fact that those who work with novices must have demonstrable knowledge and skill *in their work with those novices*. Although the state could develop such standards, without them professional practice schools might want to create and implement local performance standards for cooperating teachers. While this would not be antithetical to Connecticut's goals, it would complicate the structure of the state's program by requiring some teachers (those in professional practice schools) to meet locally set standards before they would be eligible for state compensation, while others would be compensated for similar work solely on the basis of participation in training.

The design of this reform suggests that Connecticut believed it had a quality control problem rather than a fundamental design problem (Cuban, 1988). The state did not envision changes in schools, the organization of teaching practice, or the basic preparation of teachers. Its strategy was to improve the quality of teaching within the existing organizational structure. Despite the fact that some organizational changes external to schools occurred—the creation of mandated consortia that included colleges and school districts, and teacher-dominated district committees that selected participants for training—the fundamental enterprise remained unchanged: One student teacher worked with one cooperating teacher as a culminating activity in preservice teacher education.

Connecticut's approach to reform was a set of well-integrated efforts that put it squarely in the mainstream of what Cuban (1988) refers to as "first-order" quality control.

> *First-order* changes are reforms that assume that the existing organizational goals and structures are basically adequate and what needs to be done is to correct deficiencies in policies and practices . . . solutions to quality control problems. . . . First-order changes, then, try to make what exists more efficient and effective without disrupting basic organizational arrangements or how people perform their roles. (pp. 228–229)

Connecticut's efforts to promote teacher professionalism and status through the state-designed and state-implemented mechanisms of new roles, training, and payment are predominantly a "rational planning" policy strategy, in which state control and authority over the enterprise is increased. The policy strategy by which the state is working to professionalize teaching includes increasing the role and authority of the state. Advocates of professional practice schools might suggest that this approach runs counter to their own efforts to professionalize teaching by controlling teacher education at the school level.

## Professional Development Policy in New York

Also concerned with upgrading the status and expertise of individual teachers, New York has not created state-wide, detailed, mandatory programs with which to accomplish these goals. Instead, New York has encouraged teacher development through the funding of local teacher centers, through a pilot program to support restructuring efforts, and through provision of funds for mentor programs in those districts that desire to create them. New York's current policy strategy most closely resembles what Timar and Kirp (1988) describe as a set of market incentives. The state has provided funding for specific kinds of endeavors; districts, if they have an interest in those endeavors or can meld local priorities with those of the state, can seek state funding. Furthermore, New York appears not to have defined the reform problem primarily in terms of quality control. It seems to have proceeded with what Cuban (1988) would call a "second-order" change orientation.

> *Second-order* changes . . . aim at altering the fundamental ways of achieving organizational goals because of major dissatisfaction with current arrangements. . . . [They] introduce new goals and interventions that transform the

familiar ways of doing things into novel solutions to persistent problems. The point is to reframe the original problems and restructure organizational conditions to conform with the redefined problems. (p. 229)

Policy makers and teacher educators in New York suggest that the state would like to take an active role in reorganizing authority relations in schools by promoting shared decision making at the school level. (New York State already requires its least effective school districts to involve teachers in school-site planning, recognizing the importance of local attention to needs assessment, planning, and commitment to implementation.) In its most recent commission report, the New York State Education Department (1988) fosters the idea of restructuring schools and increasing teachers' roles in decision making. The report explicitly states, "The structure now in place is failing to meet the needs of too many children" (p. 2).[5] It proposes a wide range of changes that differ from what Connecticut has in place, in that they focus on the *school*, not the individual teacher, as the unit of reform. Proposing a fund to support competitive grants to districts that want to engage in restructuring, the report recommends that districts' proposals for support should include such features as (1) joint decision making at the building level; (2) "teams of teachers working with groups of students"; (3) school-based budgeting; and (4) "alternate organization of the school day, school year, grade, and subjects" (p. 9). Nothing in New York's current restructuring plan would conflict with the formation of professional practice schools.

Three current New York staff development programs provide examples with which to consider the implications of that state's approach to policy on the growth of professional practice schools. They are: the Mentor Teacher Program, teacher centers, and the Fund for Innovation. Each is organized to encourage local program development and strategies to improve teaching and learning.[6]

**The Mentor Teacher Program.** School districts that wish to develop opportunities for experienced teachers to work with novices may submit proposals to compete for state funds under the Mentor Teacher Program. Proposals must indicate that a district committee composed 51% of teachers will select mentors, and that mentors will be released for 10% of their time and intern teachers for 20%. State funds pay for replacing mentors and interns in their classes. District committees develop their own criteria for selecting teacher-mentors. The state insists only that those selected must have taught for at least 5 years. Locally designed and implemented mentor training is required, as is evaluation of the mentoring effort. Currently, 10% (approximately 70) of the state's districts are implementing state-funded mentoring programs.[7] Given the absence of guidelines on the form and content of the components of a mentoring program, there appears to be no mismatch between this program and the kind of clinical support that might be organized in a professional practice school.

**Teacher centers.** As a way to help teachers shape their own professional development, New York began funding teacher centers in 1984. The governor introduced legislation for the centers, and New York State United Teachers worked out the detailed plans. Single districts or consortia can apply for teacher center funding on an annual basis. Centers, which are required to establish links with higher education and the business community, are governed by local boards made up of teachers representing the local bargaining agent (51% of membership), parents, representatives of higher education, industry, nonpublic schools, the school board, and local administrators. Funds are meant to supplement, not supplant, district staff development efforts.

New York has defined areas of staff development in which it has a special interest—technology, curriculum development that goes beyond state syllabi, and retraining teachers in critical areas such as math and science—but districts are free to attend to these areas as they choose. The state describes its guidelines for teacher centers as "enabling" creativity to flourish at the local level. At the moment, there are 103 teacher centers in New York, which fund, for example, grants to individual teachers that enable them to conduct research; teachers' costs associated with attending professional meetings; and collaborations between universities and teachers that might focus on content knowledge. Teacher centers can direct efforts to novice teachers, leading to programs that might intersect with mentoring efforts.

Each teacher center must conduct a needs assessment to set priorities and programs and to establish goals that will serve as the basis for evaluation. In applying for funding, centers must describe the needs assessment process, how they develop priorities, and how they assess their success. Evaluation must focus not only on individual center activities, but on the extent to which the center as a whole has met its goals. What those goals are and how they are assessed, however, is left to local discretion. The state, in reviewing proposals, looks only for the existence of a process by which this can be accomplished. As with the mentoring program, there is nothing about the organization and implementation of teacher centers from the state level that would conflict with ideas embodied in the concept of professional practice schools. In fact, teacher centers could use their funds, in collaboration with colleges and universities, to pursue staff development for new and experienced teachers that would support the creation of such schools.

**The Fund for Innovation.** New York recently created a pilot competitive grants program that is designed to approach school reform through shared decision making negotiated with collective bargaining units. The fund is encouraging schools to develop collaborative approaches to school management. Within the 14 pilot projects currently in operation, schools are working on, for example, ways to reorganize scheduling, curriculum, and multiple aspects of middle-school organization. Again, the emphasis in this program is compatible with the organization and focus of professional practice schools.

New York has intervened less than has Connecticut in creating new roles for teachers in preservice or induction-year teacher education. It provides opportunities for professional development with respect to teacher education through funding for mentor teacher programs and through its established vehicle of teacher centers. New York's reforms permit the development of varied approaches to support clinical teacher education and encourage increased teacher participation in school governance and decision making. On the other hand, because New York is using the policy model that creates artificial markets (as described above), districts are free to involve themselves in this reform or not. From the perspective of those thinking of developing professional practice schools, New York provides a policy context in which there is considerable freedom to use existing policy to support such innovation.

## School-Restructuring Efforts in Massachusetts

On a smaller scale, Massachusetts is supporting a number of programs, which, like New York, it funds through a market incentive strategy of competitive grants. Two of these programs have particular relevance for professional practice schools: the Carnegie Schools Program and the Professional Development Schools Program. Both encourage school restructuring. For those interested in the impact of policy on the creation of professional practice schools, the appropriate question is, What is the fit between state-designed restructuring efforts and the design of professional practice schools? Massachusetts provides examples with which to address that question.

The first restructuring effort is based on ideas proposed in the Carnegie Report, *A Nation Prepared: Teachers for the 21st Century* (1986). According to the *Report of the Special Commission on the Conditions of*

*Teaching* from the Massachusetts State Legislature (1987), the purposes of the Carnegie Schools Program are to

- Restructure the environment of teaching, freeing teachers to decide how best to meet state and local goals for children
- Foster professional discretion, autonomy and accountability by first providing teachers with opportunities to participate in the setting of goals for their schools and then evaluating the success of schools in achieving these agreed-upon standards of performance
- Provide a variety of approaches to school organization, leadership and governance
- Provide teachers with the support staff needed to be more effective and productive (p. 13)

The state does not have in mind one model of a restructured school that would be best for all districts, schools, teachers, or students. Rather, it is encouraging variety. Little in the Carnegie Schools Program would interfere with the restructuring that might be associated with the creation of professional practice schools. Within this funded program category, however, schools are neither asked nor encouraged to pay attention to reorganizing to improve the education of teachers. Carnegie schools are fundamentally restructured schools that attend to student learning.

The Massachusetts State Legislature (1987) created a separate policy to address restructuring issues associated with the improvement of teacher education and learning to teach. That policy encourages the creation of Professional Development Schools

in which new models of professional education are jointly designed and administered by school and college staff, in order to strengthen the role played by school-based professionals in both the initial training of prospective or new teachers and in the on-going development of experienced teachers. In addition, Professional Development Schools should ultimately forge a new partnership between schools and colleges in the operation of teacher education programs. (p. 19)

The creation of two different restructuring programs suggests that Massachusetts policy makers see a separation between *teachers'* learning and *children's* learning, a separation not present in the conception of professional practice schools. Massachusetts policy does not preclude attending to learning to teach in the Carnegie schools. The program, however, does not emphasize this domain nor does it encourage the formation of school/college collaborations for teacher education purposes.

In contrast, the Professional Development Schools Program, which awarded the first set of grants in January 1990, creates opportunities to restructure to improve preservice teacher education. This program requires the formation of school/college collaborations to restructure teacher education so that, according to the concept paper provided with the Massachusetts Professional Development School Grants Program *Request for Proposals* (1989), "the heart of future teacher education programs take [sic] place in school-based, clinical settings under the direction of school-based professionals and university faculty." Schools are free to design professional development schools as they prefer. However, the request for proposals indicates that the state is particularly interested in funding programs that address priority topics, including "inquiry-based and reflective teaching, collaboration and collegiality, . . . new organizational structures and roles that strengthen collaborative efforts." It notes that in professional development schools, school and university faculty "might pursue cooperative research, jointly plan and administer in-service programs, test new instructional models, study the applicability of research to their schools and other schools, and develop new forms of curriculum and performance evaluation and assessment, and exchange teaching roles." It appears that one could obtain funding under the Massachusetts policy to create a professional practice school.

The presence of a state-initiated program to create restructured schools that are excellent sites for learning to teach, then, will not necessarily constrain the creation of professional practice schools in that state. Policy guidelines that encourage local, collaborative program development, and leave local school/college collaborations free to determine the form and content of preservice teacher education and preparation of school-based teacher educators, might well accommodate professional practice schools. State policies that prescribe an approach to teaching, on the other hand, may prove problematic. In the case of Massachusetts, the state's preference for inquiry and reflection is in keeping with the orientation proposed for professional practice schools. Were Massachusetts to adopt the orientation to teaching in place in Florida (discussed below), state policy would play a more constraining role in the creation of professional practice schools.

## The Florida Performance Measurement System

States and districts often seek behavioral indicators of good teaching. First, they want observable data that will reliably distinguish good from poor teaching for purposes of evaluation. Second, if certain behaviors can be associated reliably with good student achievement outcomes, then novice and experienced teachers can be asked to use those behaviors and so improve their teaching. With behavioral indicators, identifying good or poor teaching requires attention only to the presence or absence of behaviors that have been identified as "effective" or "ineffective" whenever they occur, regardless of the subject, context, or students involved (Florida Office of Teacher Education, 1985).

In Florida, the research on behaviors associated with teaching effectiveness has been translated into a set of performance indicators expressed as the Florida Performance Measurement System (FPMS) and used to evaluate beginning teachers during their internship year.[8] The FPMS divides the knowledge base of teaching into six areas called *domains,* with each domain further subdivided into a set of concepts, each of which has a set of related behavioral indicators, a set of teaching principles, and a survey and analysis of relevant research findings (Macmillan & Pendlebury, 1985).

Because of its behavioral and generic orientation to teaching knowledge and performance, the requirement to teach according to the notions of effectiveness expressed on the FPMS would likely constrain implementation of the kind of teaching proposed for professional practice schools. The FPMS goes against the grain of what some would consider to be a professional orientation to teaching. The orientation proposed for professional practice schools would, according to Peterson and Comeaux (1990),

> focus on the exercise of professional judgment by the teacher, assuming that good teaching involves not only mastery of instructional behaviors and teaching techniques, but also the professional knowledge and judgment about how, when, where, and with whom to use these techniques as well as how to change and adapt them where appropriate. (p. 6)

The construction of teaching knowledge present in the Florida policy stands in stark contrast to this model, not only because it is generic and dependent on behavioral indicators rather than reflection, but also because it views outsiders—"researchers"—as the source of knowledge about teaching. The FPMS asks teachers to suspend, or never develop, their own skill and judgment about teaching, and instead to rely on the information provided by experts who study teaching. This orientation to what knowledge is and who can produce it runs counter to that proposed for professional practice schools. State policy, which mandates teachers' adherence to this conception of knowledge and teaching if they are to be certified, conflicts with the ideas central to professional practice schools.[9]

## COMPARING THE POLICIES

Each of these states is strongly committed to improving the quality of teaching and learning and is dedicating considerable human and financial resources to that goal. They differ not in their commitment, but in what they identify as stumbling blocks to improvement and in their approach to remedies.

- New York's professional development policies and proposals suggest that the fundamental design of schools is flawed and propose to restructure schools, while Connecticut accepts that organization and is choosing to improve teaching and learning in traditionally organized schools. Massachusetts is beginning to support alternatives to current organization.
- Policy makers in all four states know that teachers and schools are essential to reform. But they have created policies with different emphases. Connecticut and Florida, by their choice of improvement strategies, have emphasized the importance of individuals—teachers' knowledge, skill, and performance—while New York and Massachusetts at the moment are emphasizing schools and the conditions of teaching, learning, and learning to teach.
- Connecticut and Florida selected a body of knowledge and skill to be mastered; New York and Massachusetts have not identified the specific knowledge and skills that teachers should master, nor have they put in place formal structures in which learning should occur.
- Neither New York, Connecticut, nor Massachusetts has established performance standards for those who would support the clinical experience of preservice teachers or the mentoring of first-year teachers, regardless of the approach to support they have taken.

Each of these policy approaches has strengths and weaknesses with respect to the goals it is trying to achieve. All other things being equal, however, some policies will create greater constraints for those attempting to create professional practice schools than will others.

Policies such as those in New York and Massachusetts, by focusing on the school as the unit of reform, by encouraging local variation and collaborations with colleges, and by avoiding guidelines for the form and content of either mentoring or cooperating teacher programs or performance, provide a context in which professional practice schools could develop within the bounds of existing policies. Professional practice schools in New York could fund some of their activities through the mentor, teacher center, and Fund for Innovation programs. More limited funds are available in Massachusetts, but those that exist could be used for professional practice schools.

Connecticut, in contrast, does not have a school-based focus to its reform efforts, concentrating instead on individual teachers. It provides a context rich in policies that create organizational components and roles structurally similar to those proposed for professional practice schools, but different enough in content and source of authority that they might conflict with and complicate efforts to create professional practice schools. For example,

- A professional practice school could be developed based on a model of teaching that includes the Connecticut teaching competencies. But it is likely that such a school would seek exemptions from the craft model of teaching that places novices with *one* cooperating teacher or *one* mentor.
- Professional practice schools might want to create their own professional development programs for mentors and cooperating teachers. Questions would then, no doubt, arise about exemptions from the state's program, as they would about the state's paying mentors and cooperating teachers who did not complete the *state's* training programs.
- The consortium structure, by establishing partnerships and district catchment areas, complicates the choice of school/university collaboration partners for professional practice schools.
- The cooperating teacher program has a potentially negative impact on the possibility of creating professional practice schools because of its effect on the ability of such schools to maintain stable school-site placements over time.

This conclusion on the match between state policy context and the development of professional practice schools does not imply an endorsement or rejection of any state's policies. The purpose of the analysis is to draw attention to the kinds of state policies that exist and their implications for the creation of professional practice schools. In all states, irrespective of the policies in place, creating such schools will be difficult because the ideas, which are complicated and as yet not well-formulated, will require new ways of thinking and working for both teachers and college-based teacher educators.

## CONCLUSION

Professional practice schools would be organizations in which many long-held views on the way school and learning to teach are "supposed to be" would be transformed. Creating such schools depends, in part, on the ability of those currently engaged in teacher education and school teaching to imagine and implement new roles, responsibilities, relationships, and ideas about the nature of the work they do and the kind of organizations in which it might better be accomplished. Beyond imagining, it requires serious conversation and negotiation about issues of authority within and between schools, school districts, teachers' and administrators' organizations, universities and colleges, and state departments of education, among others. Professional practice schools imply real shifts in authority and control; as a result, negotiations and conversations will not always be easy.

At the local level, in order for professional practice schools to develop, at least the following conditions must exist:

- Desire on the part of teachers and administrators to reorganize their school so that it can become a center of inquiry focused on improved teaching and learning
- Desire on the part of classroom teachers and university-based teacher educators to work together to jointly establish a school site that is good for preservice and induction teacher education
- Organizational support *at the college and the school* for reorganizing faculty and teacher roles, rewards, and resources with respect to teacher education
- Local authority to determine the process and content of the preservice and induction-year teacher education component that will occur in the school
- Local authority to develop appropriate assessment criteria and strategies based on a conception of teaching as reflective practice

With these conditions met, it would be prudent to next consider several features of state-level policy to determine their match with the ideas central to professional practice schools. As demonstrated through policy examples from Florida, New York, Massachusetts, and Connecticut, some of these will be more conducive than others to the formation of professional practice schools. The potential to develop professional practice schools could be strong because of the absence of policies pertinent to such schools, or because extant policies urge schools in compatible directions. With regard to state influence, then, it would seem important to examine policies for the extent to which they enable or at least permit

- School reorganization with respect to students' as well as teachers' work, with respect to issues of governance as well as teaching and learning

- The development of locally conceived school/college collaborations attentive to issues of preservice and continuing teacher education
- Within such collaborations, the creation of locally designed clinical support roles for experienced teachers, including considerable local discretion around issues such as selection, preparation, and evaluation for such roles
- An inquiry approach to teaching and learning

This exploration of context at the school/university and state levels is not meant to discourage those who seek to establish professional practice schools. It is meant to convey the message that such schools will not exist in a vacuum or in an ahistorical moment in time. If we want them to have a chance to succeed, we cannot afford to ignore the importance of the environments in which we propose their growth.

## NOTES

Special thanks to Ellen Faith, doctoral candidate at the Graduate School of Education, Harvard University, for her assistance with interviews and other aspects of data collection, as well as for her insights into issues central to school/university collaborations.

1. See, for example, Holmes Group (1986), and Carnegie Forum (1986).

2. On a somewhat different theme, there is little reason to assume that liberal arts faculty would be knowledgeable about subject-matter pedagogy appropriate to students in elementary and secondary schools.

3. Lieberman and Miller's (1990) example of a teacher asking young children to describe the thought processes by which they figured out a new word in context is as much the kind of teaching that might be encouraged in professional practice schools—teaching that encourages children to construct their own knowledge and take seriously their own constructions—as it is an example of teacher inquiry.

4. As part of its comprehensive reform of teaching, Connecticut has created a mentor teacher and an assessor teacher role, along with formalizing the role of cooperating teacher. Teachers who wish to work as mentors or assessors must also complete state-developed training programs. The discussion of the cooperating teacher program is based on Neufeld (1989).

5. The report has not yet been adopted by the New York State Board of Regents; therefore, it is not state policy at the time of this writing.

6. I am grateful to Helen Hartle, Coordinator for Inservice Education in New York, for helping me obtain information about professional development programs in that state.

7. New York plans to mandate mentoring for all new teachers in 1993. Programs will still be developed locally.

8. For a review of this research, see Brophy & Good (1986); for use of the Florida Performance Measurement System, see Peterson and Comeaux (1990); for brief descriptions of state performance assessment programs for beginning teachers, see Wise and Darling-Hammond (1987).

9. Florida, as a state, is supportive of efforts to decentralize school governance to the school level. School-based management, such as that found in Dade County, is in accord with state policy. While the state has supported, with the development and implementation of the FPMS, decentralized governance structures, however, it has taken a centralized approach to policies defining effective and appropriate teaching strategies.

## REFERENCES

Brophy, J. E., & Good, T. E. (1986). Teacher behavior and student achievement. In M. C. Wittrock (Ed.), *Handbook of research on teaching* (3rd ed.) (pp. 328–375). New York: Macmillan.

Carnegie Forum on Education and the Economy. (1986). *A nation prepared: Teachers for the 21st century.* New York: Author.

Cohen, D. K. (1988). *Teaching practice . . . plus ca change.* East Lansing: Michigan State University, National Center for Research on Teacher Education. (IP88–3)

Cuban, L. (1988). *The managerial imperative and the practice of leadership in schools.* Albany: State University of New York Press.

Darling-Hammond, L. (1988). Policy and professionalism. In A. Lieberman (Ed.), *Building a professional culture in schools* (pp. 55–77). New York: Teachers College Press.

Feiman-Nemser, S., & Buchmann, M. (1983). *Pitfalls of experience in teacher preparation.* East Lansing, MI: Institute for Research on Teaching.

Florida Office of Teacher Education. (1985, June). *Summative observation instrument, Florida Performance Measurement System: Coalition for the Development of a Performance Evaluation System.* Tallahassee, FL: Author. (OTE 349)

Holmes Group. (1986). *Tomorrow's teachers: A report of the Holmes Group.* East Lansing, MI: Author.

Kennedy, M. M. (1988). Establishing professional schools for teachers. In M. Levine (Ed.), *Professional practice schools: Building a model* (Monograph No. 1) (pp. 119–153). Washington, DC: AFT.

Levine, M. (Ed.). (1988, July/August). *Radius, 1*(2). (Available from American Federation of Teachers, 555 New Jersey Avenue, N. W., Washington, DC 20001)

Levine, M., & Gendler, T. (1988). Background paper: Professional practice schools. In M. Levine (Ed.), *Professional practice schools: Building a model* (Monograph No. 1) (pp. 22–70). Washington, DC: AFT.

Lieberman, A., & Miller, L. (1990). Teacher development in professional practice schools. In M. Levine (Ed.), *Professional practice schools: Building a model, Vol. II* (Monograph No. 2) (pp. 91–120). Washington, DC: AFT.

Macmillan, C. J. B., & Pendlebury, S. (1985). The Florida Performance Measurement System: A consideration. *Teachers College Record, 87*(1), 67–78.

Manasse, A. L. (1982, March). Effective principals: Effective at what? *Principal,* pp. 10–15.

Massachusetts Professional Development School Grants Program (1989, October). *Request for proposals.* (Concept paper distributed with invitation)

Massachusetts State Legislature. (1987, August). *Report of the Special Commission on the Conditions of Teaching.* Boston: Author.

Neufeld, B. (1986). *The beginning teacher support and assessment program: Evaluation report.* Cambridge, MA: Education Matters.

Neufeld, B. (1989). *Final evaluation report: Connecticut's cooperating teacher training program—Implementation year 1987–1988.* Cambridge, MA: Education Matters.

Neufeld, B., & Haavind, S. (1988). *Professional development schools in Massachusetts: Beginning the process.* Boston: Massachusetts Field Center for Teaching and Learning, University of Massachusetts Harbor Campus.

New York State Education Department. (1988, March). *New York report: A blueprint for learning and teaching. Report of the Commissioner's Task Force on the Teaching Profession.* Albany, NY: Author.

Pechman, E. M. (1990). The child as meaning maker: The organizing theme for professional practice schools. In M. Levine (Ed.), *Professional practice schools: Building a Model, Vol. II* (Monograph No. 2) (pp. 9–90). Washington, DC: AFT.

Peterson, P. L., & Comeaux, M. A. (1990). Evaluating the systems: Teachers' perspectives on teacher evaluation. *Educational Evaluation and Policy Analysis, 12*(1), 3–24.

Schlechty, P. C., & Whitford, B. L. (1989). Systemic perspectives on beginning teacher programs. *The Elementary School Journal, 89*(4), 441–449.

Schön, D. A. (1987). *Educating the reflective practitioner.* San Francisco: Jossey-Bass.

Sykes, G., & Elmore, R. F. (1989). Making schools manageable: Policy and administration for tomorrow's schools. In J. Hannaway & R. Crowson (Eds.), *The politics of reforming school administration* (pp. 77–94). New York: Falmer Press.

Timar, T. B., & Kirp, D. L. (1988, Summer). State efforts to reform schools: Teaching between a regulatory swamp and an English garden. *Educational Evaluation and Policy Analysis, 10*(2), 75–88.

Timar, T. B., & Kirp, D. L. (1989). Education reform in the 1980's: Lessons from the states. *Phi Delta Kappan, 70*(7), 504–511.

Wise, A. E. (1979). *Legislated learning.* Berkeley: University of California Press.

Wise, A. E., & Darling-Hammond, L. (1987). *Licensing teachers: Design for a teaching profession*. Santa Barbara, CA: The RAND Corporation.

Zeichner, K. M. (1985). *Content and contexts: Neglected elements in studies of student teaching as an occasion for learning to teach*. Paper presented at the annual meeting of the American Educational Research Association, Chicago.

# About the Contributors

LINDA DARLING-HAMMOND is currently professor of Education at Teachers College, Columbia University, and codirector of the National Center for Restructuring Education, Schools and Teaching (NCREST). Her recent work has included research on teacher evaluation and selection practices, teacher supply and demand, the development of educational indicators, teacher competency testing policies, and the development of a teaching program.

HOLLY M. HOUSTON is a founder of the Center on Learning, Assessment, and School Structure (CLASS) in Geneseo, New York. CLASS assists schools, districts, and states in the design and management of change around the goals of enhanced student performance and adult professionalism. She has worked on several national reform projects, including the Coalition of Essential Schools and the National Board for Professional Teaching Standards.

MARY M. KENNEDY is director of the National Center for Research on Teacher Learning. She has conducted numerous studies on educational policies and practices and written extensively on professional expertise and on knowledge use in education.

MARSHA LEVINE is at the Geroge Washington University School of Education and Human Development, where she is directing the development of a new Institute for 21st Century Schools. She is a consultant to the American Federation of Teachers and director of the AFT Professional Practice School Project. She was codirector of the Committee for Economic Development study, *Investing in Our Children* (1985), and a consultant and Visiting Fellow in Education Policy Studies at the American Enterprise Institute. She has taught at the elementary and secondary levels and has experience in teacher education and inservice staff development.

ANN LIEBERMAN is currently president of the American Educational Research Association and a professor in the Curriculum and Teaching Department at Teachers College, where she codirects the National Center for Restructuring Education, Schools and Teaching (NCREST). She has been involved as researcher, policy maker, and practitioner attempting to build collaboration between schools and universities. Her many publications include *Teachers, Their World and Their Work* (with Lynne Miller), *Building a Professional Culture in Schools,* and *Schools as Collaborative Cultures: Creating the Future Now.*

LYNNE MILLER, Associate Professor of Education at the University of Southern Maine, has held a variety of teaching and administrative positions, most recently Assistant Superintendent of Curriculum in South Bend, Indiana. She has written many articles about life in schools, school improvement, and staff development.

BARBARA NEUFELD is president of Education Matters, Inc., a senior research associate with the National Center for Research on Teacher Learning, and a lecturer at the Harvard Graduate School of Education. Her recent work includes analysis of programs, policies, and practices designed to improve teaching and teacher education.

ELLEN M. PECHMAN is a senior research associate at Policy Studies Associates, Inc., in Washington, D.C. She was formerly a research associate at North Carolina State University and director of CATALYST, a Ford Foundation-funded mathematics improvement project. A researcher and practitioner, she collaborates with teachers, policy makers, and researchers to improve schools for both children and professionals.

# Index

171